Fred Wilson
at Oberlin

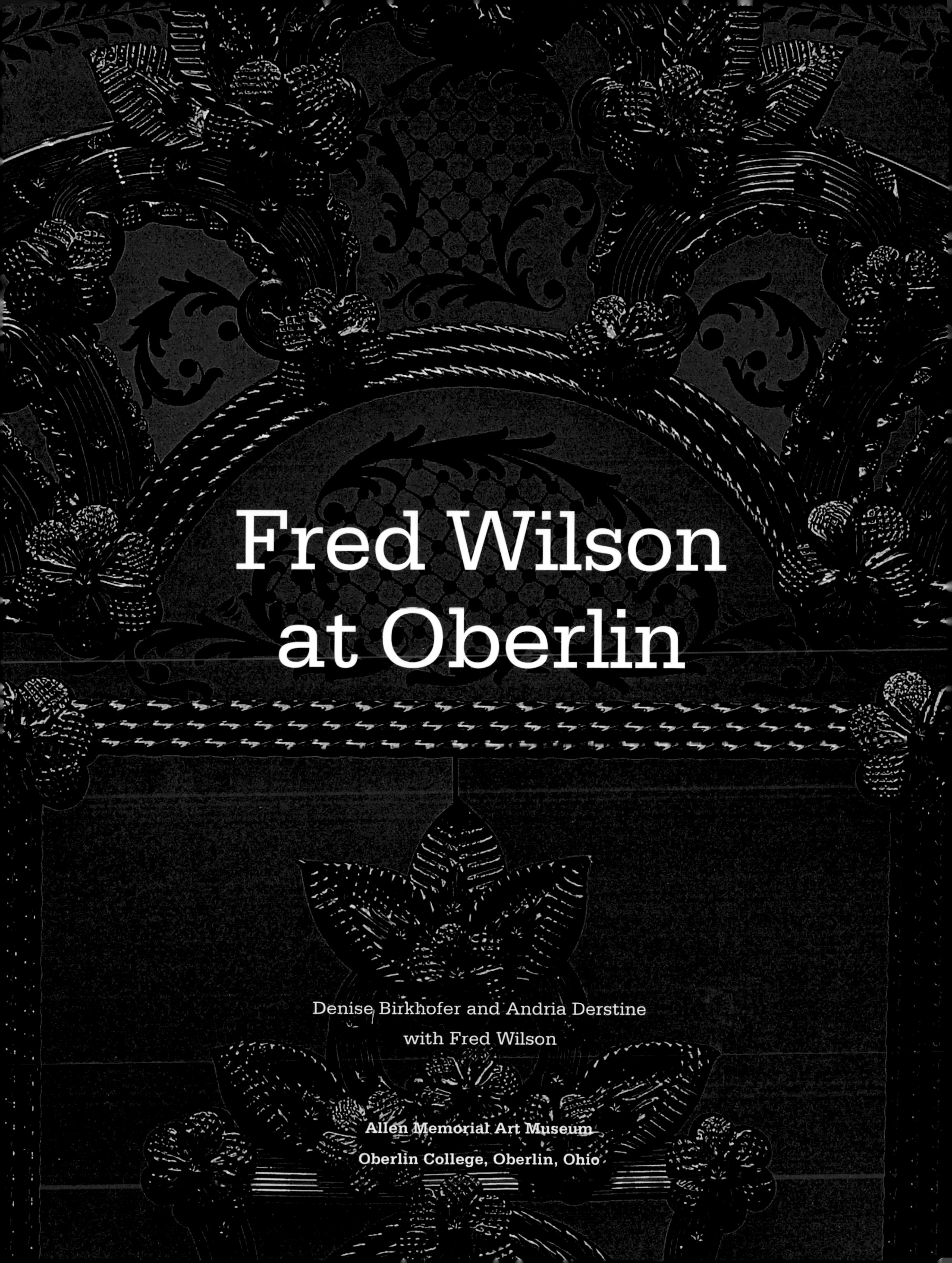

Fred Wilson at Oberlin

Denise Birkhofer and Andria Derstine
with Fred Wilson

Allen Memorial Art Museum
Oberlin College, Oberlin, Ohio

Published on the occasion of the exhibitions *Wildfire Test Pit* and *Fred Wilson: Black to the Powers of Ten* at the Allen Memorial Art Museum, August 30, 2016–June 12, 2017

Published by the Allen Memorial Art Museum, Oberlin College, 87 North Main St., Oberlin, Ohio 44074
www.oberlin.edu/amam

Produced by Lucia|Marquand, Seattle
www.luciamarquand.com

Megan A. Harding, AMAM Production Manager
Liam McLean, AMAM Editorial Assistant
Designed by Ryan Polich
Proofread by Barbara Bowen
Typeset in Serifa and Univers by Brynn Warriner
Color management by iocolor, Seattle
Printed and bound in China by Artron Art Group

ISBN: 978-0-9983831-0-1
Library of Congress Control Number: 2017933602

Frontispiece: Fred Wilson (American, b. 1954), *Bat* (detail), 2009, Murano glass and wood. Private collection.

Photography Credits
The photographs in this catalogue were taken by John Seyfried, with the following exceptions: images on the frontispiece and on pages 74–75 were taken by Kerry Ryan McFate, and are courtesy of Pace Gallery; the image on the back cover was taken by Silvia Ros.

Contents

Foreword

The exhibitions *Wildfire Test Pit* and *Fred Wilson: Black to the Powers of Ten*, shown at the Allen Memorial Art Museum at Oberlin College from August 30, 2016, to June 12, 2017, are the result of more than a year of residencies by, and conversations with, the artist Fred Wilson. Located respectively in the museum's King Sculpture Court and Ellen Johnson Gallery, the exhibitions mark the first time that two major aspects of Wilson's artistic practice have been shown simultaneously at one institution. An example of Wilson's acclaimed installations created through the "mining" of museum collections, *Wildfire Test Pit* is intimately tied to Oberlin's history. It takes as its point of departure the life of Edmonia Lewis, the important—yet for decades overlooked—nineteenth-century African American and Native American sculptor who studied at Oberlin College, and is a locus for consideration of profound, universal themes of loss and redemption. Representative of Wilson's studio practice, *Fred Wilson: Black to the Powers of Ten* presents paintings, sculpture, glasswork, prints, and a video that engage with notions of nationhood and perception. Although created with different approaches, both exhibitions seek to challenge viewers' assumptions about history, culture, and display practices, and resonate with shared notions of race, mourning, and remembrance.

Fred Wilson first visited the Allen Memorial Art Museum during the directorship of Sharon F. Patton (1998–2003). Patton, a specialist in African and African American art, greatly strengthened the museum's holdings in these areas, acquiring works by Romare Bearden, Chakaia Booker, Willie Cole, Leonardo Drew, Minnie Evans, Sam Gilliam, Rashid Johnson, Jules Lion, Robert Reid, Alison Saar, William E. Smith, Charles Wilbert White, and John Wilson, and objects from the Hausa, Igbo, Mangbetu, and Yorùbá cultures, among others. In 2002, Patton spearheaded the museum's purchase of Edmonia Lewis's *Bust of James Peck Thomas*, which centrally greets the visitor to the museum in *Wildfire Test Pit*. This 1874 bust of a former slave, sculpted by Lewis in Rome—the artist's only marble portrait of an African American whose location is known—provides a point of introduction to the exhibition's themes of memory and meaning. At Patton's invitation, Wilson first spoke at Oberlin, in Fisher Hall just behind the museum, on September 20, 2001, with a talk titled "The Silent Message of the Museum." As the attacks of September 11 had occurred a mere nine days earlier, this visit came at a loaded historical moment. All the more poignant, then, is the inclusion in *Fred Wilson: Black to the Powers of Ten* of his video *September Dream*, first shown as part of his installation *Speak of Me as I Am* at the 2003 Venice Biennale, which was, in part, a response to the attacks of September 11.

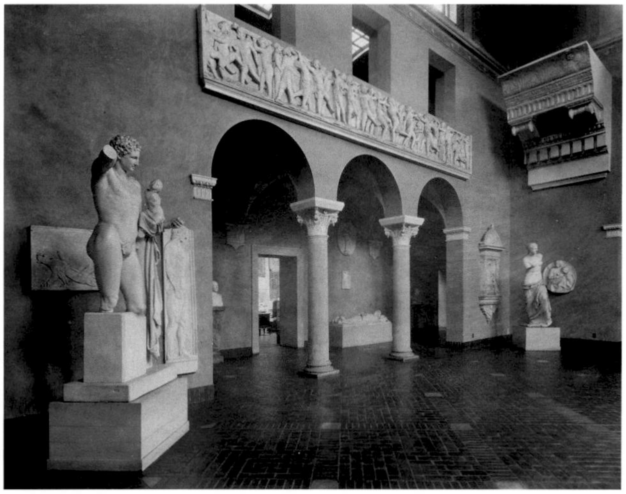

The King Sculpture Court as it appeared in the early 20th century, with plaster casts of ancient and Renaissance works.

Though he spoke in Oberlin in 2001, it wasn't until 2008 that Wilson's work was exhibited at the Allen. In that year, his *Hybrid Healing Figure*, a wooden African figure draped with four stethoscopes, was part of the spring semester iteration of the exhibition *From Africa to America*, organized by director Stephanie Wiles. In February 2013 Wilson made a second visit to the museum, when, in the company of Douglas Baxter (OC 1972 and President of Pace Gallery), we first began to discuss the possibility of a joint project—a conversation that culminated in the two powerful exhibitions this book celebrates.

While the Allen has been the venue for many site-specific installations in the past, Wilson's are especially meaningful given not only their subject matter, but also their timing. The museum celebrates its centennial on June 12, 2017, and the exhibitions serve as an ideal lead-in to a focus on and recognition of the Allen's history and collections—not least through their emphasis on both local and global history, as well as their insistence on the importance of memory and the pervasive workings of time. The inclusion in *Wildfire Test Pit* of plaster casts that were among the earliest objects displayed in the museum, in the very space they once occupied, is just one significant aspect of Wilson's work that makes clear—as his artistic practice in general so brilliantly does—the inescapable continuum that links past and present. Perhaps most inspiring is that the exhibitions highlight the crucial roles of both the artist and of the museum in the acts of creation and preservation, and in the effectuation of positive change through vision and education.

Andria Derstine
John G. W. Cowles Director

Acknowledgments

Many colleagues and supporters have contributed to make this book, and the exhibitions it celebrates, possible. We wish first to thank Fred Wilson, whose insights, creativity, and inspiring artistic vision have provided the basis for our work together. We could not have imagined a better partner, and are deeply grateful to him for his friendship and warmth of spirit. Douglas Baxter (OC 1972), President of Pace Gallery and a longstanding member of the museum's Visiting Committee, helped to arrange the first loan of a work by Wilson to the Allen in 2008, and brought him to visit in February 2013, when we first started to talk about collaborating. His contributions to the exhibitions, publication, and related programs have been manifold, and we thank him heartily for his assistance, as well as his patient good cheer.

To those who provided financial support for the exhibitions and this publication, we are especially grateful. They include Maryan (OC 1971) and Chuck (OC 1972) Ainsworth, Douglas Baxter (OC 1972), Peter Gould, Robin Potter, and Alexandra Gould (OC 2011), Agnes Gund, Karen Connors Fuson Hall (OC 1965), Suzanne Hellmuth (OC 1968) and Jock Reynolds, Charles Jonah (OC 1965), Sherida Paulsen and Steven Margulis, Betsy Pinover Schiff, Margaret C. Schultz (OC 1947), Katherine Solender (OC 1977) and Willie Katzin (OC 1974), Pace Gallery, the Ellen H. Johnson Fund for Visiting Artists, and the John H. (OC 1929) and Marjorie Fox (OC 1929) Wieland AMAM Support Fund, generously provided by John and Susan Wieland in memory of John's parents.

Many other people provided practical assistance in the mounting of the exhibitions or in other aspects of our work together, and to them we offer our deep thanks. At Fred Wilson's studio, they include Heather Bursch, Rita Campos, and

Jason Irwin; at Pace Gallery, Humphrey Bilger, Alex Brown, Justin Horne, and especially Nancy Rattenbury. Lenders to the exhibitions include Douglas Baxter (OC 1972), Nicholas Fairplay, Ken Grossi at the Oberlin College Archives, and Ed Vermue at the Oberlin College Library Special Collections. We wish also to thank John Carney, Operations Manager, Corrigan Moving Systems; Lindsey Felice, Special Collections and Preservation Assistant at the Oberlin College Libraries; Heather Galloway, conservator; Mari Kuroda, Andy Rock, and Keith Rock, who assisted in the installation; Robert Pallante at the Amherst Historical Society; Barbara Prior and Kay Spiros of the Oberlin College Clarence Ward Art Library; and Brian Hastings, Whitfield Lovell, and Alberto Zambenedetti. The staff members and security officers of the Allen Memorial Art Museum were our partners on many aspects of these projects, and we thank them for their great work and warm collegiality: Sara Banhidy, Andaleeb Banta, Selina Bartlett, Kendall Christian, Miriam Finkelman (OC 2016), Mike Gilbert, Kevin Greenwood, Megan Harding, Derrick Meyers, Liliana Milkova, Sally Moffitt, Michael Reynolds, Lucille Stiger, Christine Super, Jason Trimmer, Doug Weaver, Jim Weishampel, and, for their research assistance, Lodewijck Kuijpers (OC 2015) and Alexandra Nicome (OC 2017). We are especially grateful to registrar Lucille Stiger and preparators Kendall Christian and Michael Reynolds for their careful work in making arrangements for and installing the exhibitions, and to Megan Harding for her contributions to this catalogue. We also thank Selina Bartlett and John Seyfried for their photography, and extend our warm gratitude to the entire team at Lucia|Marquand.

We wish finally to thank the Board of Trustees of Oberlin College, President Marvin Krislov, and Dean of the College of Arts and Sciences Timothy Elgren for their advocacy of the Allen Memorial Art Museum and our many public and academic programs. Their support, and that of all of those named here, has helped to ensure that the museum continues to advance its educational mission for the good of our community.

Andria Derstine
John G. W. Cowles Director

Denise Birkhofer
Ellen Johnson '33 Curator of
Modern and Contemporary Art

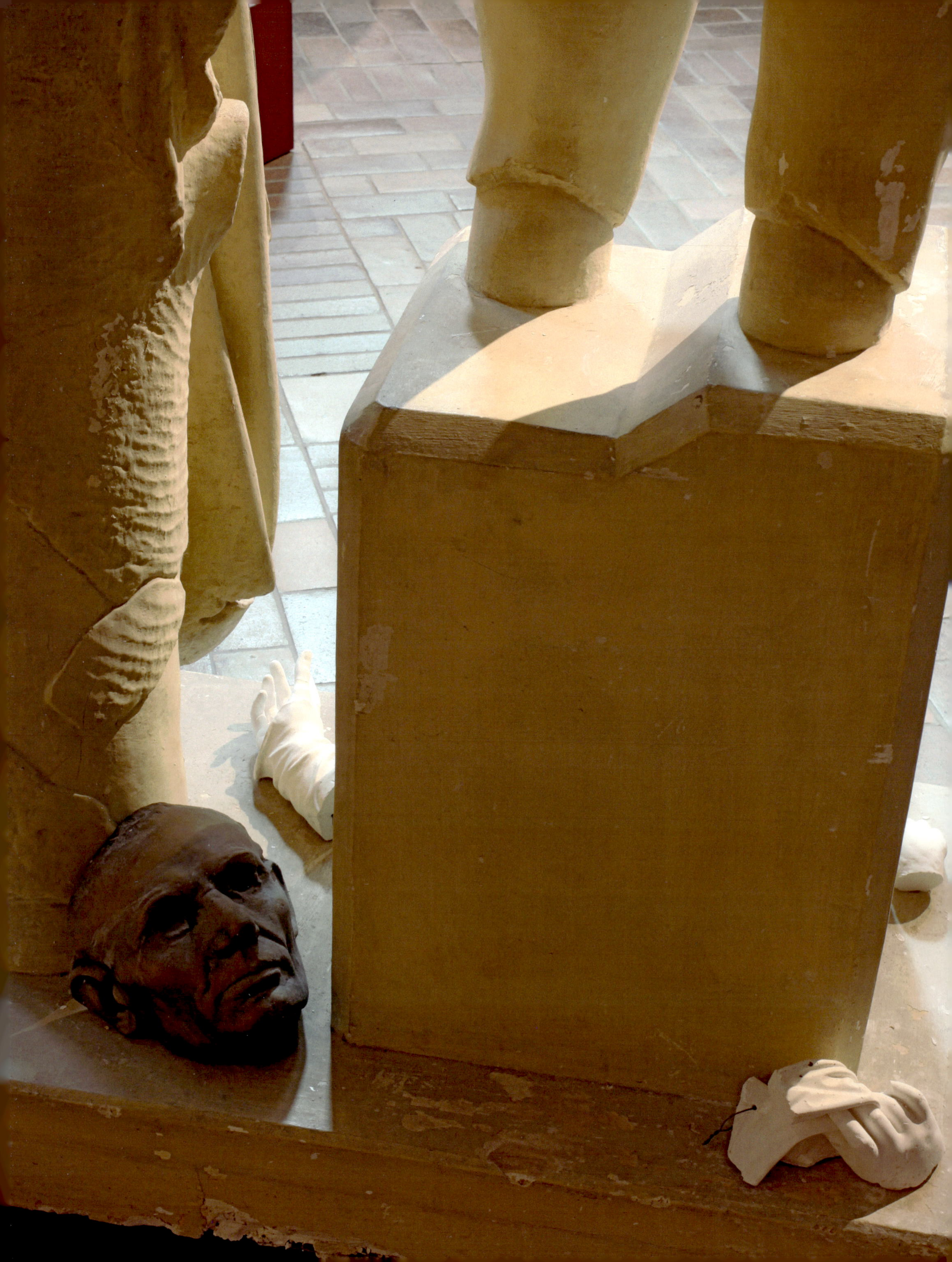

Fred Wilson at Oberlin

Wildfire Test Pit and *Black to the Powers of Ten*

Denise Birkhofer

Upon entering the main doors of the Allen Memorial Art Museum (AMAM), the visitor encounters a central gallery known as the King Sculpture Court. Named for the AMAM's curator Hazel B. King, this 1,600-square-foot space has been home to a diverse array of artworks throughout its 100-year history. Highlights from the museum's collection of nineteenth- and twentieth-century European and American art have been installed there, as well as Asian and African art. The King Sculpture Court has likewise housed temporary exhibitions spanning geographical and temporal boundaries, ranging from traditional African art to site-specific installations by contemporary artists. In 2014–15, the conservation of the gallery's faux-coffered ceiling, painted in 1917 by Frederick J. Wiley, brought the sixteenth-century French-style animal and foliage designs back to life.

Following on the heels of this century of history is Fred Wilson's site-specific installation *Wildfire Test Pit*. Culled primarily from the AMAM's collection and a number of local resources, *Wildfire Test Pit* engages with the history of the museum, Oberlin College, and the city of Oberlin. Responding to the original museum architecture, designed by Cass Gilbert, Wilson reproduces inside the gallery the inscription "The Cause of Art is the Cause of the People," from William Morris's text "Art and Socialism," which greets visitors on the museum's stone façade. He also duplicates two stanzas from the 1840 poem "Enosis" by transcendentalist Christopher Pearse Cranch, which is painted on the walls of

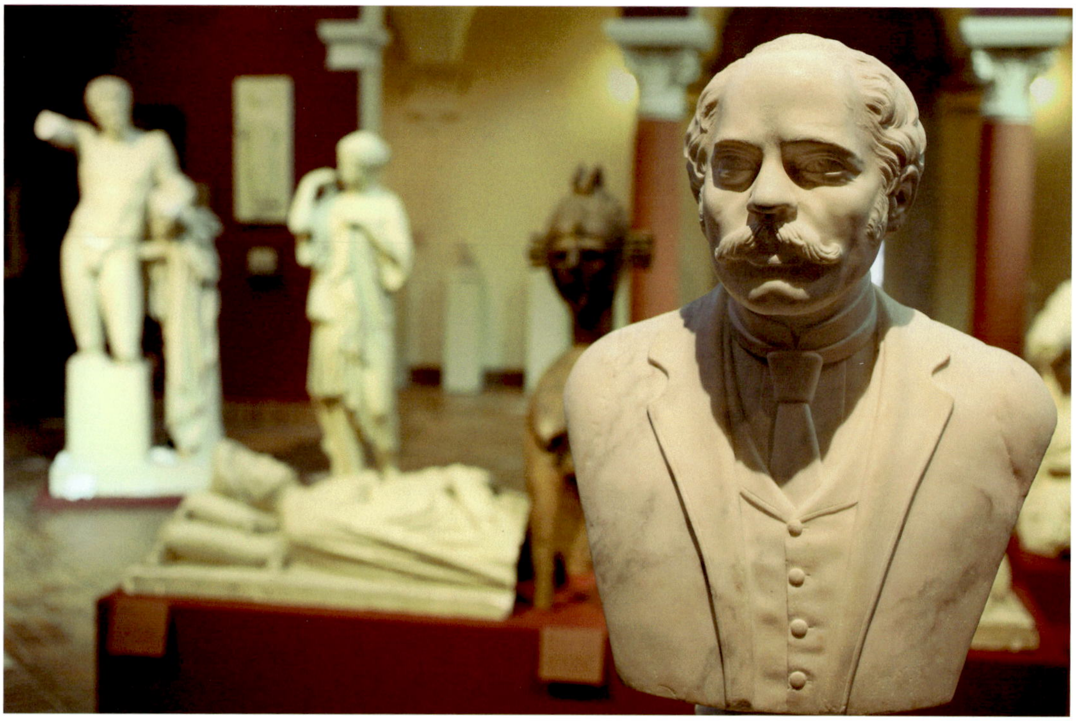

Figure 1. Edmonia Lewis (American, 1844–1907). *Portrait of James Peck Thomas*, 1874, marble. R.T. Miller Jr. Fund, 2002.3.

the clerestory.[1] Just as the ceiling and clerestory underwent the removal of a century's worth of dirt and grime by a conservation team, Wilson turns the clock back 100 years by renewing the Sculpture Court's original purpose as a site for the display of plaster casts. Purchased by Oberlin's Art Department when the museum opened in 1917, life-size replicas of classical and Renaissance works occupied this space in the earliest years of the AMAM's history (page 7).[2] Wilson selects a dozen of these casts from the museum's collection, including such well-known examples as the Venus de Milo, the Artemis of Gabii, and Donatello's *David*, and supplements these with other plaster sculptures and fragments borrowed from Oberlin-based stone carver Nicholas Fairplay. Such reproductions have been a central element of Western artistic traditions for centuries: the use of plaster casts as tools for artistic production in the ancient period was renewed by Renaissance artists, and they were widely collected by museums and art academies as teaching tools.[3] Reaching the height of their popularity as essential study aids in the mid- to late-nineteenth century, plaster casts fell out of favor around the 1930s, at which time most public institutions destroyed, deaccessioned, or removed their casts from view.[4] The AMAM's casts experienced this last fate, with the majority of the works being sent to off-site storage or to other locations such as the college's Clarence Ward Art Library. Ignored for decades and in compromised condition, the plaster casts are resurrected and restored to their original location by Wilson in *Wildfire Test Pit*.[5]

Positioned front and center among the plaster casts is a marble bust of James Peck Thomas, a former slave who went on to become one of the wealthiest black men in Missouri (fig. 1).[6] The sole stone original amid a sea of plaster casts, the bust is likewise granted prominence in Wilson's installation as the only known extant portrait of an African American subject by Edmonia Lewis, a remarkable female sculptor of mixed African and Native American descent active at the end of the nineteenth century (fig. 2). Wilson's prominent placement of the Lewis bust introduces one of the most palpable threads of *Wildfire Test Pit*, which on one level functions as a portrait of the life and work of the sculptress. Although she broke barriers of race and gender to become a successful, classically trained sculptor, Lewis did not have an easy path. After her mother's death, Lewis's father, who was a gentleman's servant, sent Edmonia to upstate New York to live with her aunts. Funds from her brother, who had become wealthy during the California Gold Rush, enabled Lewis to be educated first in Albany and then at Oberlin College. She was enrolled in the Oberlin Preparatory Department from 1859 to 1860, and in the Ladies Literary Course from 1860 to 1863. Her time at Oberlin, however, was troublesome: Lewis was accused of poisoning two white female students and was severely beaten before her trial, at which she was acquitted.[7] Abolitionists helped her move to Boston to study sculpture, and she was exhibiting her art there by 1864. After 1865 Lewis settled in Rome, where she practiced her trade as the only African American among a group of other female expatriate sculptors, producing meticulous portrait busts and other commissions.[8] Wilson's arrangement of plaster casts and other sculptural works in *Wildfire Test Pit* suggests the Roman studio (formerly occupied by neoclassical master Antonio Canova) where Lewis produced many of her most celebrated works, including the AMAM's portrait bust of James Peck Thomas. She lived out her final days in England, where she died in relative anonymity in 1907.

In addition to the bust of James Peck Thomas, Wilson includes a reproduction of a drawing by Lewis from 1862—the sole surviving example from the artist's student days at Oberlin[9]—hung high on a wall outside of the viewer's typical line of vision (page 57). By peering through a telescope located across the gallery, the composition depicting Urania, the Greek muse of astronomy, is revealed. Indicative of Lewis's enduring interest in the classical tradition, the seated figure of Urania is clad in Grecian drapery and points to a globe held in her hand, one of her common attributes. By hanging the drawing high on the wall and introducing the device of the telescope, Wilson humorously suggests Urania's association with the study of celestial objects. For Wilson, the telescope likewise serves to slow down the process of looking, forcing the viewer to pause and make a greater effort

Figure 2. Henry Rocher (American, ca. 1824–1887), *Edmonia Lewis*, ca. 1870, albumen silver print. National Portrait Gallery, Smithsonian Institution.

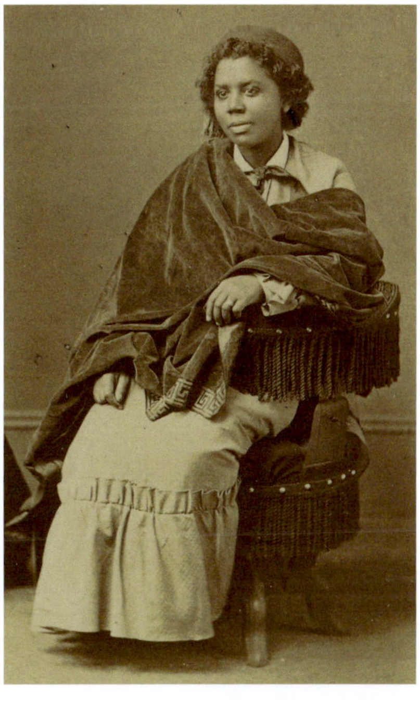

to view the image as filtered through the device. Although physically removed, the telescope lens brings Lewis's drawing right to the viewer's eye. A second telescope serves a similar function, this time fixed upon a small figure of a female spirit-spouse created by a Baule artist from the Ivory Coast (page 58). Installed on the wrought-iron balcony overlooking the King Sculpture Court on the museum's second floor, the gilded sculpture gleams from above like a sun deity or a beacon.

In addition to their celestial connotations, the Urania and Baule figures share the feminine gender prevalent in the installation. Representations of women in Western and African art from the AMAM collection relate to Lewis as a female protagonist and creator, and also stand in for the women with whom she was surrounded in her family, at school, and within her artistic circle in Rome. Plaster casts of the Venus de Milo, Artemis of Gabii, and goddesses Artemis and Aphrodite (formerly known as the "Two Fates") from the Parthenon's east pediment are presented alongside various female depictions by African makers, such as a Gelede torso mask (worn by a male performer to honor the Mother Goddess), and a Baule Kpan mask representing the most powerful female aspect of an individual's identity. In some instances, Wilson places these works in direct dialogue with one another. A Baga dance headdress representing Nimba, the goddess of fertility, is flanked by bifurcated sections of a prone plaster cast depicting the sarcophagus of fourteenth-century Italian noblewoman Ilaria del Carretto. Elsewhere, a Sowei mask made for girls' initiation ceremonies in Sierra Leone is encircled by fragments of a plaster cast taken from Andrea della Robbia's terracotta depiction of the Annunciation from the Ospedale degli Innocenti in Florence. In a cavernous space left visible between two sections of the "Two Fates" cast, Wilson similarly inserts a number of wooden West African sculptures of female figures, their bases surrounded by a pile of rock salt. By juxtaposing works of European and African origin, Wilson recontextualizes these objects and questions traditional art historical narratives.[10]

In keeping with the biographical overtones of *Wildfire Test Pit*, allusions to Lewis's ethnic background flow throughout the installation. Traditional African objects suggest her paternal roots in the continent, while late nineteenth-century works evoke the troubled and changing circumstances of African Americans during Lewis's lifetime. A painting by Thomas Satterwhite Noble (fig. 3) titled *The Present* is one of a trilogy originally intended to represent "The Past, Present, and Future Conditions of the Negro." Painted in July 1865, only three months after Abraham Lincoln's assassination and five months before ratification of the 13th Amendment abolishing slavery, Noble's composition presents a black woman on the cusp of emancipation. Seated at a smoldering hearth, she wears modest clothing accentuated by gold jewelry and an ornate shawl. The subject's ambiguous status is complicated by her confident gaze as she smokes her pipe; the shabby interior, whose floor is riddled with bones and ashes; and her foot resting on a book, a symbol of illiteracy. This moment of transition is further evoked by the wispy figure of an angel rising from the fire and a reproduction of Lincoln on the wall above the fireplace, perhaps functioning both as a eulogy to Lincoln as well as a harbinger of hope for a brighter future. Wilson further alludes to this crucial moment through the inclusion of a trompe l'oeil painting by Nicolas Alden Brooks, which depicts the handbill of the play presented at Ford's Theatre on the night of President Lincoln's assassination.

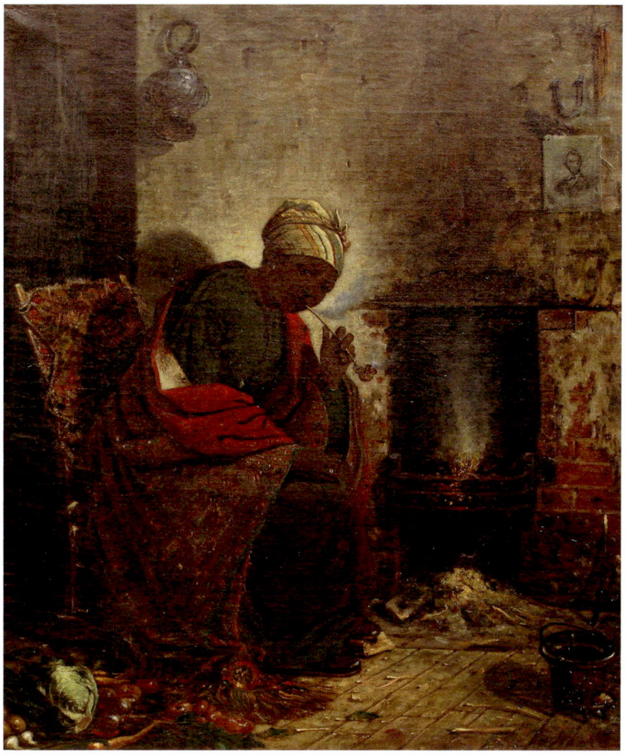

Figure 3. Thomas Satterwhite Noble (American, 1835–1907), *The Present*, 1865, oil on canvas. R.T. Miller Jr. Fund and James K. (OC 1946) and Anne Fassett (OC 1947) Sunshine American Art Fund, 2014.30.

The personage of Lincoln also provides a concrete link to Lewis's work, as she produced a marble portrait bust of his likeness in 1871, now in the collection of the San José Public Library in California. Lewis had likewise responded to the abolition of slavery in her 1867 sculpture *Forever Free*, which depicts male and female figures gazing upward, with broken chains on their wrists and ankles. Wilson makes the connection between Lincoln and Lewis all the more present in *Wildfire Test Pit* by placing a mask of the former president's visage at the base of a plaster cast installed near the Alden Brooks painting (page 10).

Despite some advances granted to African Americans coinciding with the abolition of slavery, racism continued to be an ever-present phenomenon in Lewis's United States at the end of the nineteenth century. Wilson alludes to these deep-seated biases through the inclusion of a mechanical box depicting three African American figures in a Victorian-style drawing room (page 36, center right). A mechanism is engaged when the colorful cardboard box is turned 180 degrees, causing a girl and her dog to appear to dance while musicians play in the background. The female figure is consistent with contemporary representations that promoted negative stereotypes of African Americans as lazy, greedy, mischievous, or jovial.[11] With her toothy grin and apron held out to the side, the girl is exemplary of the trope of the "dancing fool" perpetuated by the nineteenth-century minstrel show and other cultural outlets. Such problematic portrayals of African Americans were common in toys marketed to white, middle-class children in the Victorian era which served to perpetuate notions of inferiority and racial difference.[12]

The negative connotations ascribed to blackness have long been at the center of Wilson's art. In *Wildfire Test Pit*, Lewis's ethnic background becomes a jumping-off point for wider reflections on race. Installed near the mechanical box is a fifteenth-century Austrian work titled *St. Michael Weighing Souls* (fig. 4). Originally part of an altarpiece, the panel painting illustrates the winged figure of the archangel Michael, brandishing a sword overhead. His other hand supports a balance scale, indicative of his duty to weigh the souls of the dead to determine their righteousness. At one end of the scale, a fair-skinned, naked figure kneels in a gesture of piety, easily outweighing a group of demonic beings clinging to the scale's opposing cup. The corrupt souls unsuccessfully attempt to increase their heft, normally acquired through the completion of good deeds in life, by hoisting a number of heavy weights onto the scale.

Wilson likens the appearance of these weights to grindstones, and references this aspect of the composition elsewhere in *Wildfire Test Pit* through the inclusion of an actual grindstone (fig. 5). This object represents the importance of the stone-quarrying industry in Northeast Ohio: the nearby cities of Amherst and Berea, for example, are nicknamed respectively the "Sandstone Center of the World" and the "Grindstone Capital of the World." Wilson arranges small Ghanaian figurines used for the weighing of gold inside the horizontal grindstone's square hole, the tight quarters suggesting a cell or slave cabin; a solitary figure faces the stone's external edge, his nose literally "to the grindstone." Wilson further engages with *St. Michael Weighing Souls* by highlighting the figures of the "bad" souls in a number of photographic details throughout the installation, thus questioning the ascribed negative physical characteristics of the dark-skinned devils, traditional representations of evil and trickery.

Wilson has long been interested in the use of the color black in Western art to represent negative concepts such as evil or death. In an unrealized work intended for his

Figure 4. *St. Michael Weighing Souls*, ca. 1470, tempera on panel. R.T. Miller Jr. Fund, 1943.113.

Figure 5. *Grinding Souls*, 2016, sandstone grindstone and brass figures, created by Fred Wilson for the exhibition. Gift of the artist, 2016.46.1 A-K.

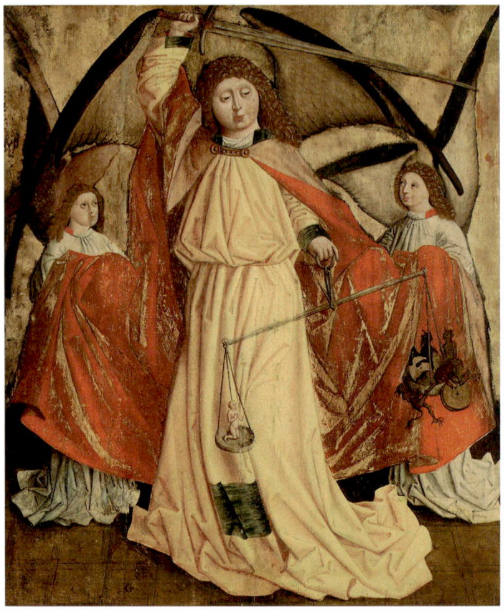

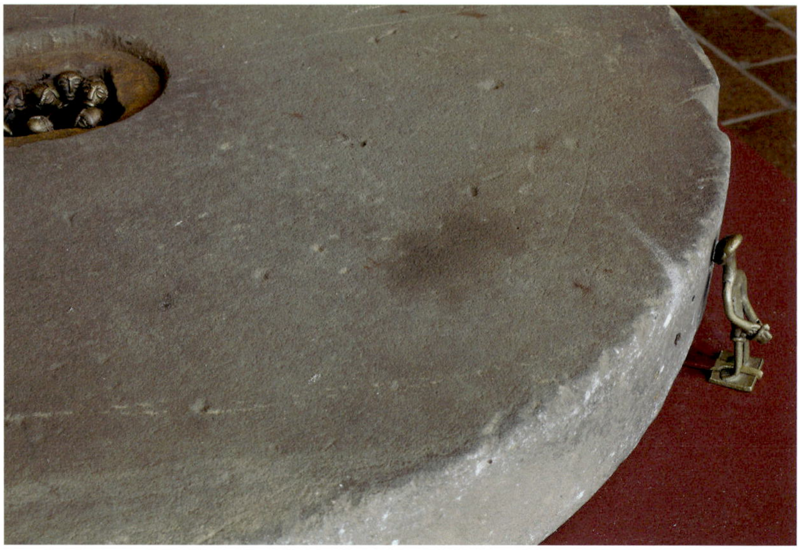

2003 installation *Speak of Me as I Am* for the United States pavilion at the Venice Biennale, the artist appropriated black devil figures from paintings of *The Last Judgment* to examine how negative stereotypes have shaped the perception of Africans in the European imagination.[13] Earlier, in his 1992 exhibition *Mining the Museum* at the Maryland Historical Society, Wilson had isolated and highlighted the figures of black slaves tucked away behind or alongside white subjects in eighteenth-century paintings through the use of spotlighting and audio recordings. In contrast to the fiendish devil figures, Wilson employs the figure of Balthazar, one of the three biblical kings to visit the newborn Christ, as a positive symbol of blackness in *Wildfire Test Pit*. At various points in the installation, the artist isolates and reproduces the head of Balthazar from an anonymous painting of the *Adoration of the Magi*,[14] thus highlighting the black king as one of the best known and most positive depictions of an African in western art and culture.

Wilson's exploration of Lewis's ethnicity in *Wildfire Test Pit* extends beyond notions of blackness. In addition to her African American heritage, Lewis bore Native American ancestry as her mother, Catherine, was claimed to be part Chippewa (also known as Mississauga Ojibwe):

> My mother was a wild Indian and was born in Albany, of copper color and with straight black hair. There she made and sold moccasins . . . Mother often left her home and wandered with her people, whose habits she could not forget, and thus we, her children, were brought up in the same wild manner. Until I was twelve years old, I led this wandering life, fishing and swimming . . . and making moccasins.[15]

This aspect of Lewis's upbringing is evoked through the inclusion of two pairs of Sioux and Cheyenne moccasins from the turn of the century, displayed near floor level to suggest their use. The leather slippers, embroidered with multicolored beads in decorative patterns, represent the Chippewa customs and crafts that Lewis would have learned from her mother. Her Chippewa background continued to influence her artistic interests later in life, as she frequently chose Native American themes as subjects for her marble sculptures, most notably in a series of works inspired by Henry Wadsworth Longfellow's epic poem *The Song of Hiawatha*.[16] The title of Wilson's installation, *Wildfire Test Pit*, refers to Lewis's self-proclaimed Chippewa name, "Wildfire," a fitting epithet for such a vital and talented personality.[17]

While not intended as a biographical narrative of Lewis's life and its accompanying trials and triumphs, Wilson's installation does suggest the suffering she experienced during her time at Oberlin. On the southeast wall is a large plaster cast of a Grecian-style stele representing the allegorical figures of Rectitude and Love. For Wilson, the classical pair functions as a stand-in for the two white, female students who falsely accused Lewis of having poisoned them, while the positioning of the stele below Lewis's drawing of *Urania* (page 57), executed at Oberlin, further underscores the context of her student days. To the right of the stele, George Segal's sculpture *Black Girl, Black Doorframe* is tucked into a corner. The life-size figure, a rare painted-black example as opposed to the artist's signature white, adopts a vulnerable stance: emerging from the dark doorway, she gazes downward with her arm clasped tightly across her body. Segal's subject becomes a surrogate for Lewis and the persecution she suffered while at Oberlin: cowering away from the looming allegorical figures, she turns inward. In the center of the Sculpture Court, plaster casts of David with the head of Goliath by Verrocchio and Donatello (the latter wittily standing over an arrangement of severed plaster "heads") symbolize Lewis's underdog status and ultimate triumph, overcoming obstacles of race and prejudice to become an internationally successful artist.

The mistreatment that Lewis suffered as a student is a particularly troubling episode in Oberlin's past, proof that the town's progressive reputation—especially in terms of race relations and gender equality—has not always rung true. While rightfully shedding light on this dark moment, Wilson also fleshes out other more honorable aspects of local history. The first in the nation to admit both students of color and women, Oberlin College has long been recognized as a bastion for inclusiveness and liberal values. These sentiments were widely shared by the nineteenth-century founders and later citizens of the city of Oberlin, who exhibited fervent support for abolitionism and operated an active program of assistance for escaped slaves heading north to freedom on the Underground Railroad. Wilson refers to Oberlin's anti-slavery legacy through the inclusion of a bronze bust from the collection of the Oberlin College Archives by French sculptor Joseph-Charles de Blézer of John Brown (1800–1859), an abolitionist who advocated violent opposition to slavery. Although primarily operating out of New England, Brown spent part of his childhood in Hudson, Ohio, and his father, Owen Brown, served as a member of the Oberlin Collegiate Institute's Board of Trustees from 1835 to 1844. Oberlin College students Samuel S. Burdett and Henry P. Kinney joined Brown in the "Bleeding Kansas" campaign against slavery supporters in 1856, while Oberlin residents John A. Copeland, Lewis Sheridan Leary, and escaped slave Shields Green participated in Brown's unsuccessful raid on a federal arsenal at Harper's Ferry, Virginia, in 1859. Leary died of a wound received in the raid, and Brown, Copeland, and Green were captured and hanged. Edmonia Lewis made several works of her own depicting John Brown, beginning with a series of medallions in the 1860s and a portrait bust made in Rome in the 1870s.[18] Wilson pairs Oberlin's bronze bust of John Brown with lyrics from Nina Simone's moving 1964 protest song "Mississippi Goddam," creating a link between historical and more contemporary instances of racial oppression and social unrest.

A similarly tragic episode in Oberlin's history of antislavery activism is represented in *Wildfire Test Pit* by the weathered gravestone of a young boy (page 37), now in the Oberlin College Library Special Collections. In March of 1853, a slave woman named Miriam arrived in Oberlin with her family, having fled their master in Kentucky upon learning that her daughters were to be sold.

They brought with them a four-year-old foster child named Lee Howard Dobbins, who had become extremely ill by the time the group arrived in Oberlin. As Miriam's family could not risk waiting for his convalescence, the child was left in the care of an Oberlin family as the others continued to safety in Canada. Dobbins died of consumption a week later. The whole town mourned his death: a thousand people reportedly flocked to Oberlin's First Church for his funeral, where all grieved not only the loss of this child, but the horrors of slavery.[19]

Installed near the gravestone in *Wildfire Test Pit* is the terracotta sculpture *Head of a Negro* by African American sculptor Richmond Barthé. The individualized portrait study of a young black boy functions as a stand-in for the lost Dobbins, a relationship that Wilson makes explicit in a corresponding text that reads "Head of a Boy/ Head of an African American Boy/ Portrait of an African American Boy/ Portrait of Lee Howard Dobbins." A bench positioned in front of the arrangement provides visitors with a space to pay their respects.

The funereal connotation conferred by the young Dobbins's headstone reverberates throughout *Wildfire Test Pit*. The plaster cast of the stele representing Rectitude and Love is a reproduction of a 1917 marble memorial located in Lake View Cemetery on the plot of the Prentiss family, a prominent Cleveland family and in-laws of the AMAM's founder, Elisabeth Severance Allen Prentiss. On the opposite wall, the painting *Ethiopia* by self-taught, Cleveland-based African American artist Reverend Albert Wagner features a display of grief, as the crowned queen at the center of the composition weeps for the uncrowned figure at the right edge of the picture plane, for he has not yet realized God's omnipotence (page 41). The figure of the Ethiopian queen in this work ties into the exhibition's recurrent themes of race and women, while the artist Wagner provides yet another connection to the Northeast Ohio region. Elsewhere in the gallery, *Negro Family* by Belgian painter Angèle Watson portrays a familial group that seems to be in mourning: well-dressed in black clothing, the seated figures clasp their hands properly in their laps and cast their eyes downward in a somber expression (page 52). The black family unit stands in for the foster family of Lee Howard Dobbins, as well as that of Edmonia Lewis.

Wilson extends the context of mourning to Lewis's story throughout the installation, not just in recognition of the persecution that she endured in life, but also the negligence suffered by her legacy in death. Following a successful artistic career in Rome, where she supported herself largely by the sale of commissioned portraits, Lewis lived out her final days in relative anonymity near a convent on the outskirts of London. She fell into obscurity after her death in 1907, and the date and place of her death, as well as the location of her burial, remained unknown until recently discovered by scholar Marilyn Richardson.[20] Her work largely disappeared from the public eye until interest in her legacy was renewed starting in the late 1980s, due to the research of a select group of scholars.

Some of Lewis's best known works went missing, such as the AMAM's *Bust of James Peck Thomas*, whose location was unknown after it left the possession of the sitter's daughter; it eventually turned up in an antique shop shortly before it was purchased by the museum in 2002. Even more dramatic is the story of Lewis's 1876 marble sculpture *The Death of Cleopatra*, whose whereabouts were unknown until it was rediscovered in the early 1980s (fig. 6). Anomalous from the majority of artistic representations that tend to highlight the dramatic moment of the Egyptian queen's suicide by snake bite, Lewis's sculpture depicts Cleopatra's slumped and lifeless body after the moment of death.

Although not physically present in *Wildfire Test Pit*, *The Death of Cleopatra* becomes an unseen protagonist, its trajectory paralleling many of the exhibition's central themes. Sometime after being exhibited at the Philadelphia Centennial Exposition in 1876 and the Chicago Interstate Industrial Exposition of 1878, the sculpture was acquired by "Blind John" Condon, a noted Chicago gambler and racetrack owner, whose favorite horse was also named Cleopatra. Condon placed *The Death of Cleopatra* as a memorial to his horse when the animal was buried on the grounds of his Forest Park racetrack, a fitting counterpart to the funereal subtext permeating *Wildfire Test Pit*. The sculpture remained in place when the land was made first into a golf course in 1911, and then a naval ordnance plant in 1942.[21] When the post office took over the site in the 1970s, *Cleopatra* was removed and sent to a salvage yard. There it was discovered in a severely damaged condition by Harold Adams, a local fire inspector.[22] It was thereafter brought to the attention of the Forest Park Historical Society, which acquired the sculpture in 1985 and, after a period of limbo that included temporary relocation of the sculpture to a local shopping mall, subsequently donated it to the Smithsonian Museum of American Art in 1994, where it underwent extensive conservation treatment.[23] *Cleopatra*'s story also includes an Oberlin chapter, as the sculpture was on view in the AMAM's galleries on extended loan from 2001 to 2004.

Wilson's *Wildfire Test Pit* is a metaphor for the process of unearthing Edmonia Lewis's obscured legacy and the rediscovery of her work. The exhibition's title refers not only to Lewis's proclaimed Chippewa name, Wildfire, but also suggests an archaeological connection through the use of the term "test pit," also known as a "test trench," a method used in initial surveys of archaeological sites to check for the presence of cultural materials. The tall, symmetrical, and darkly painted walls encircling the King Sculpture Court evoke a pit-like space, its floor littered with various cultural remnants. Sculptural fragments scattered around the bases of the plaster casts call to mind the site of a dig. In contrast to an idealized and timeless view of the classical world as depicted in Giorgio de Chirico's painting *La Solitudine*, on view nearby, the plaster casts of Greco-Roman originals reveal the ravages of time, their surfaces marred and crumbling. Wilson likens the damage incurred by these works to the violence inflicted upon Lewis at Oberlin and the posthumous neglect of her artistic legacy. The poor condition of the plaster casts also evokes the deterioration of Lewis's sculptures when they languished away from the public eye.

In addition to suggesting the degradation caused by indifference, Wilson calls attention to distinct, harm-inflicting occurrences: lines of text positioned high on the walls in *Wildfire Test Pit* reproduce excerpts from museum correspondence relating to slight damage that occurred to Lewis's *Cleopatra* when it was transported to the AMAM from the Smithsonian Museum of American Art in 2001. Wilson combines part of a letter to the museum's registrar relating the episode with excerpts of accounts of the poor condition in which *Cleopatra* was rediscovered in Illinois. The subject of Wilson's text shifts ambiguously from *Cleopatra* to Lewis herself with the phrase "...lying in the cold, her clothing torn and her body terribly beaten," lifted from a report of Lewis's assault, the whole creating a vivid picture of the suffering endured by the artist and her works alike. This text is mingled in the installation with other phrases derived from journalistic or scholarly sources that discuss Lewis's life and works, as well as strategically placed smaller texts appropriated from footnotes of writings by scholars Kristen P. Buick, Susan Crowe, Patricia Hills, Juanita Marie Holland, and Harry and Albert Henderson, which offer snippets of further insight into Lewis's biography and historical context.[24]

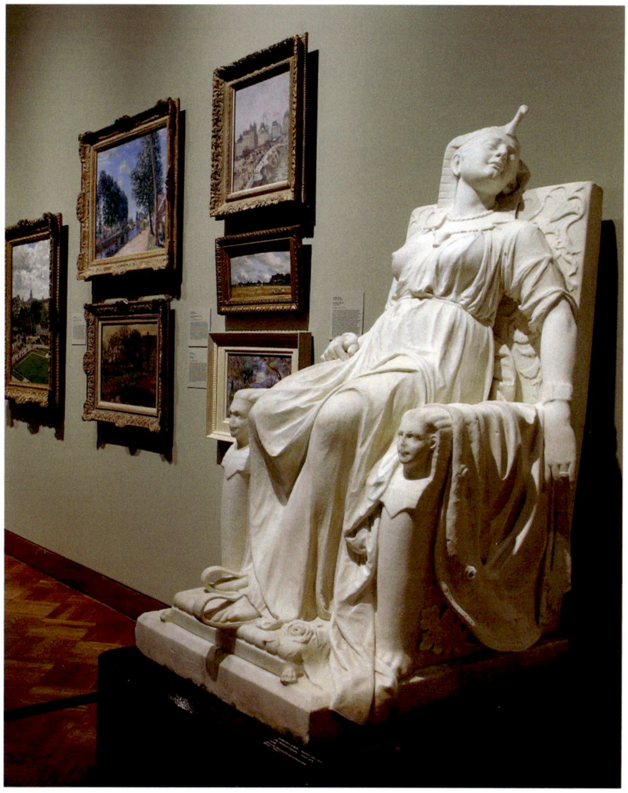

Figure 6. Edmonia Lewis's *The Death of Cleopatra* installed in the exhibition *Figure to Non-Figurative: The Evolution of Modern Art*, curated by Stephen D. Borys at the Allen Memorial Art Museum, August 23, 2002–June 9, 2003.

Exemplified by the recovery and restoration of *The Death of Cleopatra*, the "excavation" of Lewis's legacy and works, as symbolized in *Wildfire Test Pit*, is not only that of scholars and art historians, but also that of Wilson personally. As much as the exhibition addresses the obscuration and revelation of histories over time, it is likewise about Wilson's personal process of discovering Lewis's story. Over the course of his museum residency, Wilson's research on her life and work revealed many parallels with his own life: beyond shared ethnic and artistic backgrounds, a particularly striking coincidence is the fact that Wilson's paternal grandmother was named Urania, the mythological subject of Lewis's Oberlin drawing. The archaeological metaphor of discovery is also analogous to Wilson's artistic approach, which has frequently been compared to that of an archaeologist: Jennifer Gonzalez, for example, has referred to Wilson as a "Foucauldian archaeologist" who "unearths" objects to reveal hidden histories and the internal ideologies of cultural institutions.[25] Wilson himself exploited the archaeological metaphor in his choice of a title for the 1992 exhibition *Mining the Museum*, which evokes an image of the artist sifting through dusty underground caverns to uncover unknown treasures.

As in *Mining the Museum* and other previous projects with institutional collections, in *Wildfire Test Pit* Wilson highlights objects normally hidden away in museum storage. He places at center stage in the AMAM's most prominent location many works that have not recently been (nor are likely to be) featured in the galleries by curators. These works—such as the less-than-pristine plaster casts, the nineteenth-century mechanical box, and the unattributed *Adoration of the Magi* painting—occupy an awkward place in the AMAM collection due to their compromised condition, lesser quality, or anomalous character. Wilson emphasizes these anomalies in support of the exhibition's message about ruin and redemption: violating one of the central guidelines of museum best practices, he puts works in need of conservation treatment on public view as reminders of the effects of time. Just as many of Lewis's sculptures were forgotten and later brought to light, Wilson has recovered neglected objects from AMAM storage. An early nineteenth-century work by American painter Washington Allston, for example, depicts an unfinished oil sketch of a lively tavern scene, the composition heavily obscured by water damage (page 43). Also in need of repair is a small fifth-century stucco Buddha from Afghanistan; removing the broken figure, Wilson chooses to display only the sculpture's empty wooden mount (page 53). The contours of the figure eerily accentuate its absence, while also calling to mind the contemporaneous Buddha statues that were destroyed in Afghanistan's Bamiyan Valley by the Taliban in 2001. Previously withstanding centuries of weathering and other external forces, the empty silhouettes of the colossal Buddhas are a testament to the impact of willful human iconoclasm.

Wilson conceived of *Wildfire Test Pit* as a vehicle to explore the chaotic events of the contemporary world. The exhibition's prevalent themes of ruin and decay are paralleled by the mass destruction of cultural property by fundamentalist groups in the Middle East, perhaps best exemplified by the Islamic State's recent campaign of devastation in Syria. The marred condition of the AMAM's plaster casts suggests the detrimental impact on the region's archaeological sites. The turbulent aspects of Lewis's story, represented by her beating as a student and the accidents befalling her artworks, likewise symbolize the seeming upsurge in violence occurring across the globe, marked by government coups, terrorist attacks, and mass shootings. It is nearly impossible to look at the dancing girl in the Victorian mechanical box or at George Segal's *Black Girl in a Black Doorframe* in relation to Lewis's beating without calling to mind the Black Lives Matter movement, which was founded in 2013 in response to the systemic persecution and violence against black people in the United States and abroad. These events have had a particular impact on the students and community at Oberlin College, whose political awareness and commitment to social justice has been publicly manifest in recent years.

Wilson's *Wildfire Test Pit* does not propose solutions to these troubling issues, but instead offers a space for reflection and catharsis. Yet a glimmer of hope is present via the exhibition's theme of redemption, exemplified by the recovery and restoration of *The Death of Cleopatra* and the renewed scholarly interest in Lewis's artistic contributions. Wilson likewise offers a means of defense against the world's ills in the form of a mass of rock salt spilling out of an overturned metal trash can (fig. 7). The salt refers to the symbolic function of this element in some African diaspora communities, where it is used as a spiritual cleanser or to remove evil energy from a space. Wilson attaches to his arrangement a museum label for a plaster cast (present in an earlier iteration of the exhibition's checklist) of the *Apoxyomenos*, an ancient Greek sculpture depicting an athlete removing grime from his body, whose name derives from the Greek verb meaning "to clean oneself." The salt cleanses the exhibition space and offers protection against bad omens, such as the breakage suffered by *The Death of Cleopatra*; encircling the base of the AMAM's marble bust of James Peck Thomas, a salt barrier prevents such a fate from befalling that work.

The inclusion of salt crystals in *Wildfire Test Pit* is Wilson's response to the AMAM's *Slant Piece* by Robert Smithson, one of the Post-Minimalist artist's signature "nonsite"

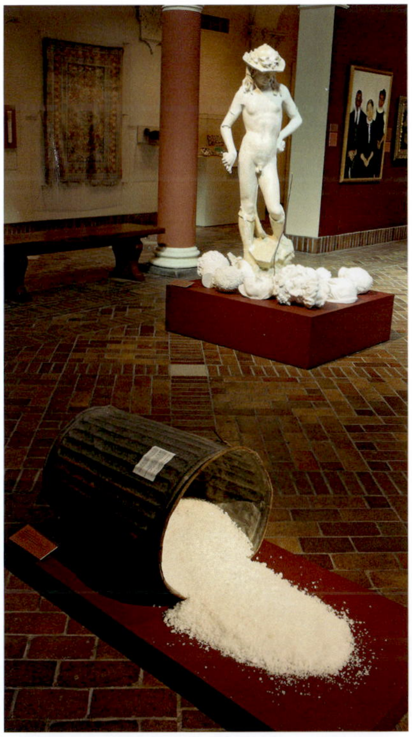

Figure 7. Foreground, *The Apoxyomenos*, 2016, metal trash can and rock salt, created by Fred Wilson for the exhibition. Gift of the artist, 2016.46.2 A-B.

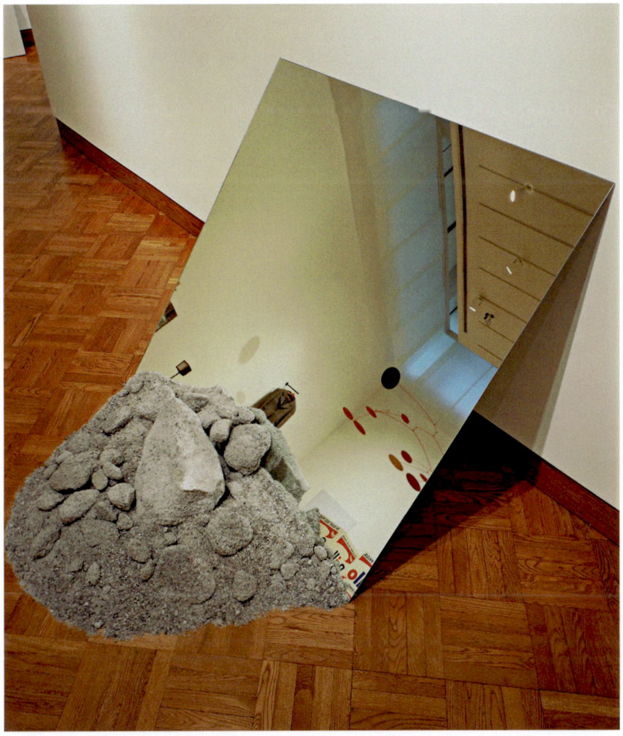

Figure 8. Robert Smithson (American, 1938–1973). *Slant Piece*, 1969–76, mirror and rock salt. Gift of the Buckeye Trust in memory of Ruth C. Roush (OC 1934), 1980.22.

works, made up of rock salt piled on the floor in front of a square mirror leaning against a wall (fig. 8). Wilson was inspired by the unceremonious way in which the rock salt for *Slant Piece* is stored in a Rubbermaid garbage can in the museum's basement. His recreation of the trash can of salt is both a playful look behind the scenes of the museum as well as a witty homage to Smithson, who was an important artistic influence on Wilson in his youth.[26] As Smithson's rock salt was originally quarried from a specific salt mine, Wilson's use of salt refers once again to the importance of the local Ohio stone industry, also represented by the grindstone. The salt connects the components of *Wildfire Test Pit* in a continuum that originates locally and extends outward, linking the salt in the ground below us to the celestial bodies in the heavens, represented by the Baule "sun deity" and the goddess Urania visible through the telescopes.

Concurrent with works that come primarily from the AMAM's collection in *Wildfire Test Pit*, the exhibition *Black to the Powers of Ten* presents works by Fred Wilson in the AMAM's Ellen Johnson Gallery. Featuring glass works, paintings, sculpture, prints, and a video made between 2003 and 2014, the exhibition explores concepts of race, time, and memory that run parallel to the themes of *Wildfire Test Pit*.

The title of Wilson's exhibition, *Black to the Powers of Ten*, refers to the short documentary films *Powers of Ten* by Charles and Ray Eames (1968 and 1977), which examine the universe on its most macro and atomic levels. Released in its final version in 1977, the film places humanity at the center of its examination, wedding scientific observation to existential anxieties about humankind's role in the cosmos. The film begins with the camera parallel to the ground, revealing one square meter of space from a distance of one meter: a couple relaxes on Chicago's lakeshore after a lovely picnic. Traveling backward on a logarithmic scale based on a factor of ten, and reaching a new increment every ten seconds, the square frame encompasses ever wider areas of space, quickly losing sight of planet earth and pausing only when arriving at the end of the observable universe, roughly midway through its nine-minute running time. From this vertiginous observation point 100 million light years away from the initial sunny patch of grass, the camera then snaps back, reversing its direction and plunging quickly back to earth. As if to quell the overwhelming sense of irrelevance elicited in the viewer, the film then turns to an examination of the minuscule, traveling at the speed of the negative power of ten, thereby slowing down its observation at each increment until it reaches the building blocks of all matter, the quarks in a proton of a carbon atom (0.00001 angstroms). While it relativizes the human ambition for dominion over what is seen and unseen, the film also comforts the viewer by showing the interconnectedness and interdependence of the micro with the macro, ultimately resorting to measurements based on the observable world, such as earth's proportions (the meter), and the circadian rhythm (the second). As with the *Vitruvian Man* of Leonardo da Vinci, the *Powers of Ten* documentaries center on humanity's cognitive and physical (in this case, perceptual) abilities to comprehend the cosmos.

The breadth of Wilson's concerns parallels the scope of the Eames films, from the ultra-local to the global. The themes of *Black to the Powers of Ten* reflect the vastness of space and time, ranging from individual to universal concerns, and addressing time periods from prehistory to the present day. A series of works inspired by the flags of African nations—many established during the same time period in which the film was made—are representative of the use of visual iconography as a means to codify and comprehend the earth and its people. On a smaller scale, in his black mirrors Wilson plays with optics to engage individual perception as a method to understand the world, a tactic paralleled by his use of the telescope in *Wildfire Test Pit*.

The juxtaposition of the macrocosmic and the microcosmic in the *Powers of Ten* films is also present in a series of six prints by Wilson. Created during a 2004 residency at Crown Point Press, the prints make extensive use of spit bite aquatint as well as other intaglio techniques to achieve rich tonal areas. Dripping acid onto an etching plate from varying heights, Wilson created splotched marks of different sizes, a method that paralleled his interest in the properties of black liquids, such as ink and oil, which likewise permeated his contemporary experimentation with black glass "drips" and "drops." The resulting clusters of spots resemble celestial bodies or organisms in a petri dish, simultaneously evoking the cosmic and the molecular. Wilson personifies the spots through the incorporation of dialogue written by white authors in the voice of black literary characters. Accompanying speech bubbles on three of the compositions reproduce quotes from characters in diverse works of literature, creating a space for them to speak with one another. The title for *We Are All in the Gutter, But Some of Us Are Looking at the Stars* is a quote spoken by the character of Lord Darlington in Oscar Wilde's *Lady Windermere's Fan, A Play About a Good Woman*, while *Arise!* derives from dialogue spoken by William Shakespeare's Othello, a central point of inspiration for many of Wilson's works in *Black to the Powers of Ten*: "Arise, black vengeance, from hollow hell!" The voices in *Exchange* appear to discuss themes of love and relationships. Other lines—penned by such celebrated writers as Herman Melville, Norman Mailer, and Eugene O'Neill—hint at negative metaphors for darkness or blackness, a recurrent theme in Wilson's work ("The tragedy will lie in the color black!;" "I fear your sparkling darkness"). A line spoken by Tituba in Arthur Miller's play *The Crucible* ("You lie, devil, you lie!") connects to Wilson's exploration of representations of the black devil also found in his interpretation of the fifteenth-century painting *St. Michael Weighing Souls* in *Wildfire Test Pit*.

Historical perceptions of blackness are also a central component of *The Mete of the Muse* (2006), which juxtaposes two bronze figures: a white-painted nude in the Greco-Roman style and an Egyptian figure with a black patina (page 81). In pairing these two works, Wilson questions assumed notions of the origins of European and African culture and civilization. The black sculpture reproduces an eighteenth-dynasty Egyptian representation of the Goddess Nephtys, daughter of Osiris and Isis, from the collection of the Louvre, while the white counterpart is a Praxitelean Venus Anadyomene figure, a popular and widely diffused Greco-Roman type that exists in well-known versions in the Vatican and other public collections. Wilson cast his figures from copies of copies of original works; his bronzes were made from plaster cast versions that he purchased respectively at an antique shop and plaster cast studio in New York City.[27] This multi-tiered removal from the primary context suggests the mutations that can occur with the passing down of tradition.

Wilson's title epitomizes the dialogues that are introduced through the artistic devices of juxtaposition and copying. The word "mete" can be defined as a limit, boundary, or boundary stone. Wilson was likewise interested in the word's more archaic meaning, which is related to the contemporary Dutch word *meten*, meaning, "to measure." Muse refers to a classical European view of artistic inspiration. A visual comparison of the countenances of the two "muses" reveals the boundaries between them: while their histories are intertwined, their differences remain. For Wilson, his artistic inspiration derives from such subtle similarities and (especially) the differences, or boundaries, between cultures that remain unnoticed or unexamined.

As in *The Mete of the Muse,* Wilson made a bronze sculpture from a plaster cast in *Ota Benga* (2008). This bust replicates a plaster cast that Wilson encountered in 2005 while creating his installation *So Much Trouble in the World* at the Hood Museum of Art at Dartmouth College. The original bust was cast from life from a twenty-three-year-old Bachichi man named Ota Benga, who was taken from the Belgian Congo and put on display along with representatives of other ethnographic groups at the 1904 World's Fair in St. Louis. At the Hood, Wilson installed the plaster bust of Ota Benga at the end of a row of other life casts taken of persons from various ethnic groups at the fair, where it was the only representation to be identified as a particular individual.[28] In *Black to the Powers of Ten, Ota Benga* stands alone in front of Robert Venturi's *Ironic Column* visible beyond a large window (page 79), flanked by two of Wilson's ornate black mirrors and a suspended chandelier. With a piece of white silk, Wilson obscures the ethnographic label, which reads "PYGMY," that was prominent on the original cast. He adds text on the base—its height approximate to Ota Benga's stature of four feet eleven inches—that reads "I'm the one who left, and didn't come back." The words suggest what Ota Benga might have said to his Bachichi community had he had the chance to speak to them. Wilson's presentation honors the memory of Ota Benga and the hardships he suffered. Following the World's Fair, he was sent to the Bronx Zoo where he was displayed in a cage with an orangutan, and later was transferred to an orphanage. Unable to return to Africa, Ota Benga committed suicide at the age of thirty-two.

As in Wilson's figurative sculptures, notions of race and blackness are explored in two-dimensional works in *Black to the Powers of Ten* that adopt the flag as a form of representation that is often taken for granted. In these paintings, Wilson removes the color from the flags of African and African diaspora countries, leaving behind only the black lines, shapes, and symbols. Each composition maintains the proportions of the original flag from which it is adapted, the graphic elements outlined in black acrylic on raw canvas. These works question the notion of the flag as a static representation of a country, and address what Wilson refers to as the "unfinished business of nationhood in many of these countries."[29] A selection of thirty-five flags is installed in a grid-like arrangement in *Black to the Powers of Ten*, the negative areas and symbols of each canvas creating interesting visual juxtapositions with its neighbors. Installed to the right in a corresponding grid format are wooden plaques that mimic institutional wall labels of the United Nations and governmental displays of the 1950s. The inscribed texts describe the history of each flag, the symbolism of the removed colors, and the significance of its imagery (pages 80–81).

The grid is also the central organizing structure of *The People* (2010), a long, horizontal painting presenting a visual index of flag symbols in which the color black represents the citizens of specific communities (page 63). Wilson isolates black imagery from the flags of twenty-seven African, African diaspora, and South Pacific nations, thus bringing together a disparate body of people through iconography. In *Black Birds* and *Black All Stars* (2014), Wilson isolates only star or bird iconography, rendering these symbols onto a canvas surface in the same location where they would have been positioned on their respective flags. *Black Birds* retains the traditional horizontal format of a flag, while *Black All Stars* is rotated vertically. The overlapping icons are related to Wilson's frequently used artistic device of layering, an approach also found in his mirror sculptures. While this technique has many possible meanings, in his paintings Wilson views it in relation to time: the compression of time, simultaneity of world events, or divergent philosophical understandings of time. In his 2012 work *LIBERATION*, Wilson focuses on just one flag: the Pan-African flag, also known as the Black Liberation flag.[30] The green and red colors are removed, leaving only the central black stripe on a raw canvas (page 76).

LIBERATION, which recently entered the AMAM collection, combines Wilson's flag imagery with his signature blown glass forms, with which he first experimented during an artist residency at the Pilchuck Glass School near Seattle in 2001. The glass "drips" appear to seep from the bottom of *LIBERATION*'s canvas like black liquid. Simultaneously liquid and solid, Wilson's drips are ambiguous natural forms evoking tears, blood, oil, or ink. The color black invites the viewer to ruminate on the connotations of blackness as a material and as a descriptor of race, while the opaque surface reflects the surroundings. Wilson arranges his glass drips as configurations of drops that appear to ooze from the wall and sometimes pool onto the floor in puddles, as in *Drip Drop Plop* (2001). In *Whether or Not* (2014), on view in *Black to the Powers of Ten* (pages 74–75), the glass forms of various sizes are clustered into three groups, two of which seem to cascade off to the side as though guided by a heavy wind.

Wilson had engaged with the material of black glass and with the symbolism of oil and ink in the earlier works *Black Memory* (2005) and *Black Present* (2006). Located in the center of the Ellen Johnson Gallery, these two wooden vitrines (page 77) are outfitted with panels of black glass to complicate the viewer's attempts to see the contents inside, partially reflecting the outside world instead. A close look reveals an array of empty glass inkwells and metal oil canisters, evoking the black liquids (ink and oil) they once contained. These objects suggest the history of the use of these liquids, including the global consequences of the oil economy and the legislation, treaties, and conflict directives signed to carry out the plans of a powerful few that affect the powerless many. In *Black Present*, these elements are accompanied by an artificial skeleton (page 66), which grants the vitrine a coffin-like appearance. Wilson previously made use of encased plastic skeletons in *The Last* and *Friendly Natives* (1991), in which he labeled the figures with such designations as "The Last Ancestor" and "Someone's Sister," suggesting the loss of individuality and personal history that occurs when human remains are displayed as artifacts in a museum.[31] The old-fashioned wooden vitrines of *Black Memory* and *Black Present* similarly evoke the display aesthetic of the natural history museum, while the modular black glass conversely recalls the clean lines of minimalist sculpture.

Wilson's relationship with the medium of glass developed further when he began to work in collaboration with glassblowers on the Venetian island of Murano in preparation for the 2003 Venice Biennale. His solo exhibition in the United States Pavilion, *Speak of Me as I Am*, focused on the subject of Shakespeare's character Othello, the Moor of Venice, as a stand-in to examine the role of Africans in Venice from the Renaissance period to the present. Stemming from his interest in the representation of Africans in Venetian fine and decorative arts, Wilson collaborated with glass artisans to create updated versions of traditional Italian decorative objects, such as chandeliers and mirrors, in black glass. Playing with traditional Venetian designs, Wilson often alters the scale and color of his creations but maintains their decorative and structural elements. As in the drips and the vitrines, the black color renders the glass both opaque and reflective, while also evoking connotations of race and mourning.

Black to the Powers of Ten features one of Wilson's Venetian-style chandeliers and three mirrors. The smallest mirror in the exhibition at 45 inches tall, *Bat* (2009) features ornately contoured panels of glass layered on top of one another and trimmed with etched patterns and foliage designs. Equally intricate but of substantially different design is *I Saw Othello's Visage in His Mind* (2013), titled after a line spoken by Desdemona early on in Shakespeare's play, in which Othello's white Venetian wife declares her love for him. The title of the largest mirror, *Act V. Scene II – Exeunt Omnes* (2014), refers to the final stage direction in *Othello* in which all characters exit, leaving only an empty expanse of stage (page 82).

Suspended above the mirrors *Bat* and *Othello's Visage* is the black glass chandelier *No Way But This* (2013). Wilson conceived of the black chandelier (page 78) in the context of his Venice Biennale installation, where its ornate luxury and color evoked contrasts between European empires and the fate of African people. The hybrid design of *No Way But This* introduces anachronistic spherical orbs and cups from the mid-twentieth century to an eighteenth-century Venetian design. Like many of the black glass works, this chandelier's multivalent title is derived from *Othello*, spoken by the protagonist at the moment of his suicide upon learning that evidence of the adultery of his wife Desdemona had been fabricated.

The sole example of video in *Black to the Powers of Ten* likewise adopts the fictional character of Othello as its focal point (fig. 9). Originally shown on four synchronized monitors in Wilson's Venice Biennale project, *September Dream* adapts footage from four opera and film productions of Shakespeare's *Othello*, in which the role of the Moor is played by white actors wearing varying degrees of blackface. On the top left is a clip from the 1951 modernist masterpiece *Othello*, starring and directed by Orson Welles. Opposite is an excerpt from a 1965 filmic production of a play by the National Theatre of Great Britain, starring a young Maggie Smith as Desdemona and a sickly colored, overly dramatic Laurence Olivier as the titular character. Below are two filmic adaptations of Giuseppe Verdi's opera based on the Shakespeare play: Franco Zefirelli's 1986 *Otello*, starring the great Spanish tenor Plácido Domingo, and a 1958 version directed by Franco Enriquez for Italian television and starring Mario Del Monaco and Renato Capecchi. Wilson focuses on the climactic death scene in each film, editing and reversing the final sequence where Othello kills Desdemona. Through its disruption of traditional narrative structure, *September Dream* questions notions of history and nostalgia while also addressing themes of race and violence. The title of the video refers to the aftermath of the terrorist attacks on the United States on September 11, 2001, relating the story of Othello to a contemporary context of mourning. Wilson has referred to this work as "...an immediate response to my unrelieved sadness after September 11. It is a fantasy, however futile, about restoring the world to the way it was before the tragedy."[32]

Figure 9. Fred Wilson (American, born 1954). Still from *September Dream*, 2003, four-channel digital video. Courtesy of the artist.

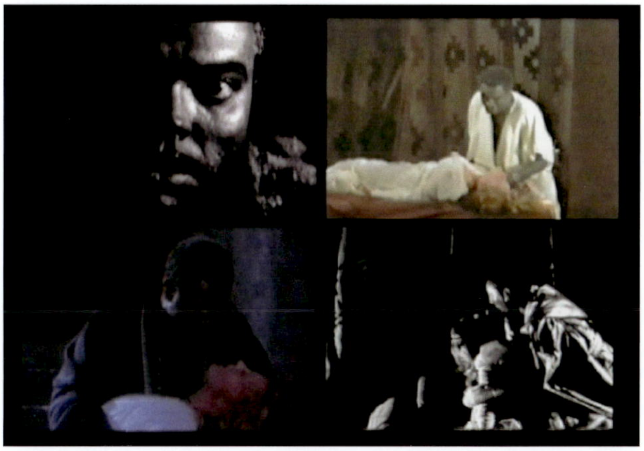

Although intended as two distinct projects, Fred Wilson's *Wildfire Test*

Pit and *Black to the Powers of Ten* are united by common themes, such as visual perception and the questioning of perpetuated notions of blackness. The role of the sculptural figure in the Western artistic tradition is central to both: the passing down of classical models via the plaster cast in *Wildfire Test Pit* is paralleled by *The Mete of the Muse*'s discourse on the copy in *Black to the Powers of Ten*. An Italian context also permeates throughout, present in the Greco-Roman casts, Edmonia Lewis's academic training and Roman workshop, and the Venetian context of Wilson's Othello-inspired, Murano glass creations. Even more telling than these thematic overlaps is the shared artistic approach behind *Wildfire Test Pit* and *Black to the Powers of Ten*: in both exhibitions, Wilson explores the "lacunae of history" (to use Maurice Berger's words) to reveal difficult truths about the present.[33] The stories of historical individuals Edmonia Lewis and Ota Benga, for example, are unearthed as starting points for the discussion of wider issues relating to race, oppression, and legacy. Both installations offer a space for reflection on the tragedies of the past and the problems of the present, while subtly inspiring hope for recovery and redemption.

1. Wilson reproduces the first stanza of a poem by Christopher Pearse Cranch (1813–1892): Thought is deeper than all speech,/ Feeling deeper than all thought;/ Souls to souls can never teach/ What unto themselves was taught. He also includes the third stanza: Heart to heart was never known;/ Mind with mind did never meet;/ We are columns left alone,/ Of a temple once complete. These lines hint at some of the currents flowing through *Wildfire Test Pit*, including pedagogy, the human body, and the classical tradition.

2. "As We Were – 1917." *AMAM Bulletin XXIV*, no. 1 (1966), 44. Many of the AMAM's plaster casts were produced by the Boston-based Italian master craftsman Pietro Paolo Caproni (1862–1928), who made molds directly from prized originals in major museum collections around the world.

3. "Digital Sculpture Project: Adolf Borbein, 'On the history of the appraisal and use of plaster casts of ancient sculpture,'" 2009. Accessed July 21, 2016. http://www.digitalsculpture.org/casts/borbein/.

4. Anthony Grafton, Glenn W. Most, and Salvatore Settis, eds. *The Classical Tradition* (Cambridge: The Belknap Press of Harvard University Press, 2010), 733–34.

5. Wilson has worked extensively with plaster casts in the past due to his interest in the copy as a loaded fragment of history. His 1992 sculpture *Artemis/Bast*, for example, shown in the exhibition *Panta Rhei: A Gallery of Ancient Classical Art*, combined plaster reproductions of the head of the Egyptian god Bast and the body of the Greek goddess Artemis. Wilson later featured many casts in his 2005 installation *So Much Trouble in the World—Believe it or Not!* at Dartmouth College's Hood Museum of Art, including a series of life-cast busts made from individuals exhibited as representations of various ethnic groups at the 1904 World's Fair in St. Louis (see page 79). Wilson's sculpture *The Mete of the Muse* was similarly produced from plaster cast models (see page 81).

6. Susan Crowe, "Visual Narratives and the Portrait Busts of Edmonia Lewis" (Kansas City: University of Missouri-Kansas City, 2010), 12. James Peck Thomas (1827–1913), a successful businessman, was born a slave in Nashville, Tennessee. His mother bought his freedom, and he then successfully petitioned for the right to remain in the state, something no previously freed African American had been allowed to do. Thomas later moved to St. Louis and, through real estate speculation and an advantageous marriage, became one of the wealthiest African Americans in the city. In 1873, Thomas met Lewis in her studio in Rome and commissioned the AMAM's bust.

7. At Oberlin, Lewis lived at the house of Reverend John Keep, a respected trustee and supporter of women's rights, where she was the only non-white boarder among a group of eleven other female students. Although accounts differ, in January of 1862, Lewis was accused of poisoning fellow boarders Christina Ennes and Maria Miles. While on a sleigh ride, the girls became violently ill with stomach cramps. Suspicion pointed to Lewis, who had served them hot spiced wine in her room earlier that day. Charges were filed, but before the trial a group of unknown individuals took justice into

their own hands and beat Lewis nearly to death, leaving her in the snow to die. After a lengthy recovery, the case was dismissed pre-trial and all charges were dropped. Lewis returned to school, but was unable to graduate due to a subsequent accusation of stealing art supplies. Rinna Evelyn Wolfe, *Edmonia Lewis: Wildfire in Marble* (Parsippany, NJ: Dillon Press, 1998), 24–40.

8. Wilson reproduces on the gallery wall the names and life dates of these female artists, as well as a list of the known subjects of whom Lewis made portrait busts.

9. Wolfe, 24.

10. Maurice Berger has referred to Wilson's juxtapositions as "activist allegories." See "Viewing the Invisible: Fred Wilson's Allegories of Absence and Loss," in *Fred Wilson: Objects and Installations, 1979–2000: Issues in Cultural Theory*, 4 (Baltimore: University of Maryland, Fine Arts Gallery, 2000).

11. Christopher P. Barton and Kyle Somerville, "Play Things: Children's Racialized Mechanical Banks and Toys, 1880–1930," *International Journal of Historical Archaeology* 16, no. 1 (February 21, 2012), 62.

12. Ibid.

13. Salah Hassan, "Fred Wilson's *Black Venezia*: Fictitious Histories and the Notion of Truth," in *Speak of Me as I Am* (Cambridge: List Visual Arts Center Massachusetts Institute of Technology, 2003), 40.

14. *The Adoration of the Magi* likewise provides another link to Lewis's body of work, as she was commissioned in the early 1880s to create a now-lost marble bas relief of the subject for the Chapel of St. Mary's in Baltimore. Holly Solano, "Evidence of Edmonia Lewis's Lost Work Found in Baltimore Church." *Artfix-Daily*, February 4, 2011. http://www.artfixdaily.com/artwire/release/5021-evidence-of-edmonia-lewis%E2%80%99s-lost-work-found-in-baltimore-church.

15. "Miss Edmonia Lewis," *Lorain County News* (April 4, 1866), 3.

16. Lewis and Longfellow met once in person in Rome during the winter of 1868–9. She made a marble portrait bust of Longfellow in Rome in the early 1870s. Timothy Anglin Burgard, *Edmonia Lewis and Henry Wadsworth Longfellow: Images and Identities* (Boston: Harvard University Art Museums, 1995), 2.

17. Wolfe, 15.

18. Upon seeing a bust of John Brown by the sculptor Edward Augustus Brackett, one of Lewis's teachers in Boston, Lewis reportedly remarked that "a man who made a bust of John Brown must be a friend of my people." Ibid., 42.

19. Purchased with funds collected at the funeral, the stone bears the following inscription: Let slavery perish! LEE HOWARD DOBBINS A fugitive Slave orphan brought here by an adopted mother in her flight for liberty MAR. 17, 1853. Left here wasted with consumption, found a refuge in death MAR. 26, 1853 Aged 4 Years.

20. "Sculptor's Death Unearthed: Edmonia Lewis Died in London in 1907," *Variety, Spice, Life* (January 9, 2011). https://artandhistory.wordpress.com/2011/01/09/edmonia-lewis-died-in-1907/.

21. Ron Grossman, "2 Saviors vie for *Cleopatra*," *The Chicago Tribune* (June 20, 1988), 5.

22. Ibid. Adams later recalled that upon his discovery of *The Death of Cleopatra*, ". . .she was like a big white ghost lying out there between all that heavy machinery and crying out to be saved." With the help of a boy scout troop, Adams reportedly retrieved the sculpture from the salvage yard and attempted to fix it up himself, cleaning off graffiti and applying a coat of white paint.

23. Smithsonian American Art Museum, "Cleopatra: Lost & Found," online exhibition, accessed August 8, 2016. http://americanart.si.edu/exhibitions/online/lewis/intro.html.

24. See Kristen Pai Buick, "The Sentimental Education of Mary Edmonia Lewis: Identity, Culture, and Ideal Works," Ph.D. diss. (University of Michigan, 1999); Susan Crowe, "Visual Narratives and the Portrait Busts of Edmonia Lewis," Master's thesis (University of Missouri-Kansas City, 2010); Patricia Hills, "Cultural Racism: Resistance and Accommodation in the Civil War Art of Eastman Johnson and Thomas Nast," in *Seeing High and Low: Representing Social Conflict in American Visual Culture*, edited by Patricia Johnston (Berkeley and Los Angeles: University of California Press, 2006); and Juanita Marie Holland, "Mary Edmonia Lewis's *Minnehaha*: Gender, Race, and the 'Indian Maid,'" in *Diaspora and Visual Culture: Representing Africans and Jews*, edited by Nicholas Mirzoeff (London and New York: Routledge, 2000).

25. Jennifer Gonzalez, "Against the Grain: the Artist as Conceptual Materialist," in *Fred Wilson: Objects and Installations*, 29.

26. Author's conversation with the artist, August 2016. Wilson shares with Smithson an interest in elemental materials, fragmentation, entropy, time, anti-materialism, and the mirror as a perceptual device. Wilson has spoken of his black glass drip works as "the operatic version of Smithson's cinema verité," positioning the drama of his elemental black glass as a counterpart to the unassuming quality of Smithson's natural materials such as salt or dirt.

27. Ibid.

28. Barbara Thompson, "Making So Much Trouble in the World," in *Fred Wilson: So Much Trouble in the World—Believe it or Not!* (Hanover: Hood Museum of Art, Dartmouth College, 2006), 19.

29. "Fred Wilson at Frieze New York," press release, May 2016, http://www.pacegallery.com/exhibitions/12806/frieze-new-york.

30. Now part of the Allen Memorial Art Museum collection, purchased in 2016 through the Ruth C. Roush Contemporary Art Fund and a partial gift of the artist and of Pace Gallery, Douglas Baxter (Oberlin College '72), President.

31. Huey Copeland, "Out of the Well," in *Fred Wilson: Black Like Me*, exh. cat. (Ridgefield, Conn.: The Aldrich Contemporary Art Museum, 2006), 25.

32. Kathleen Goncharov, "Interview with Fred Wilson," in *Fred Wilson: Speak of Me as I Am*, 24.

33. Berger, 10.

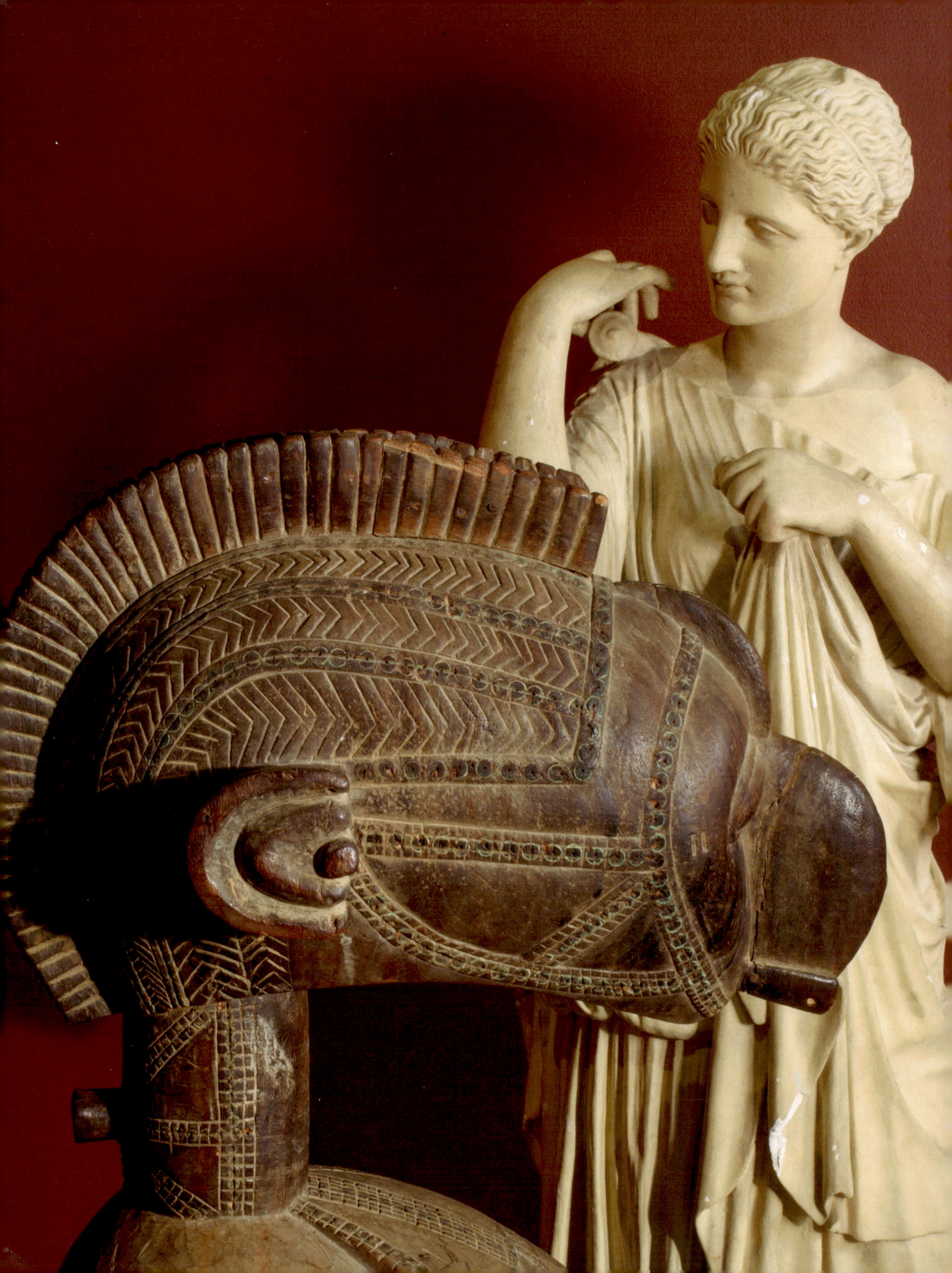

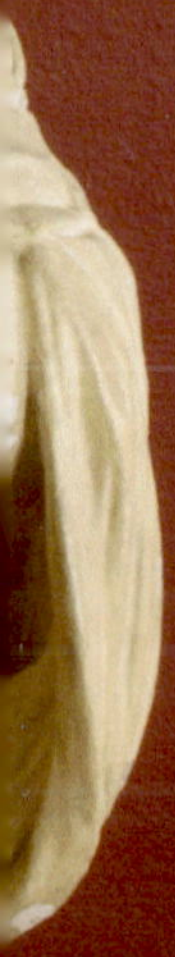

Wildfire
Test Pit

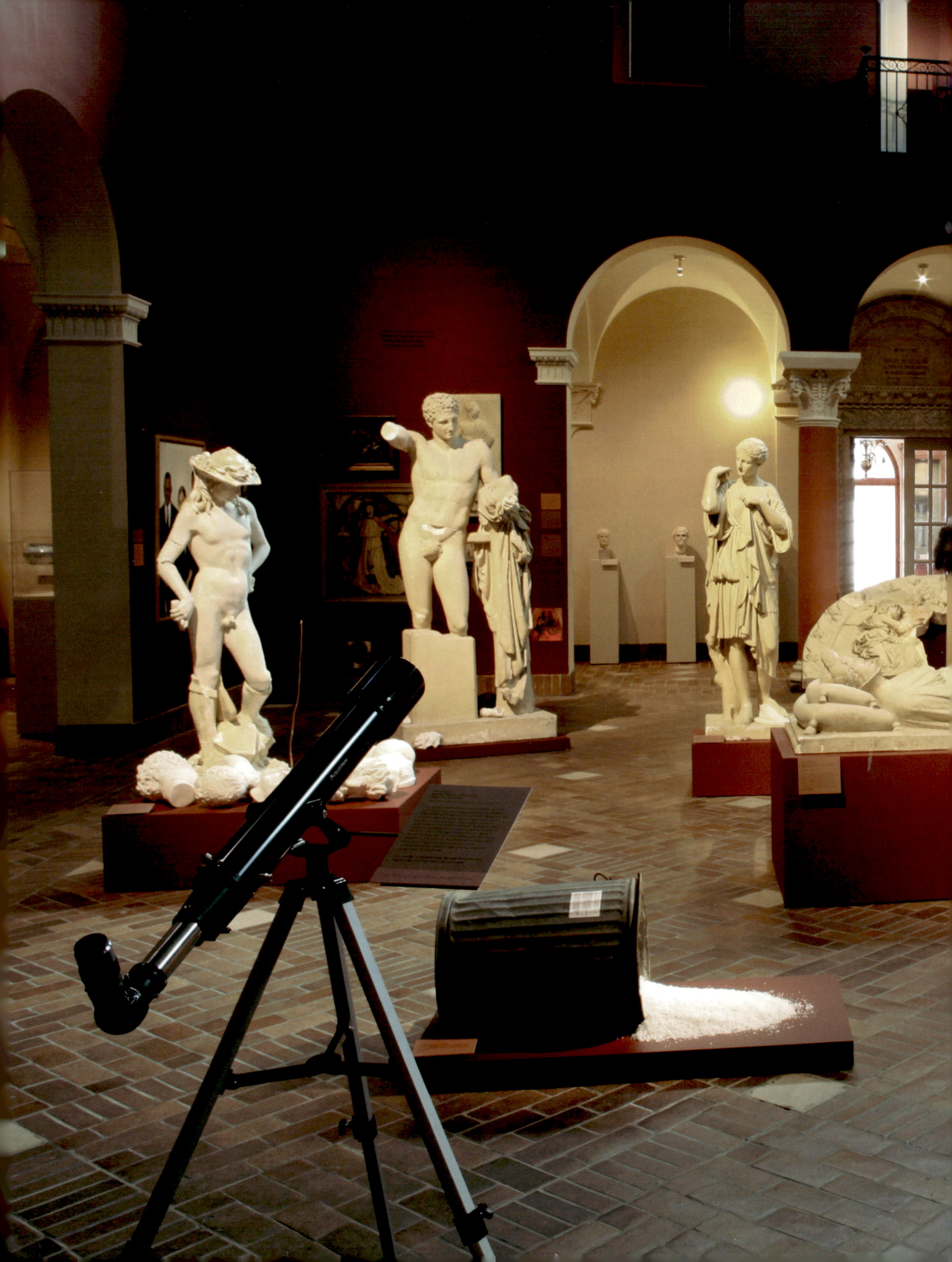

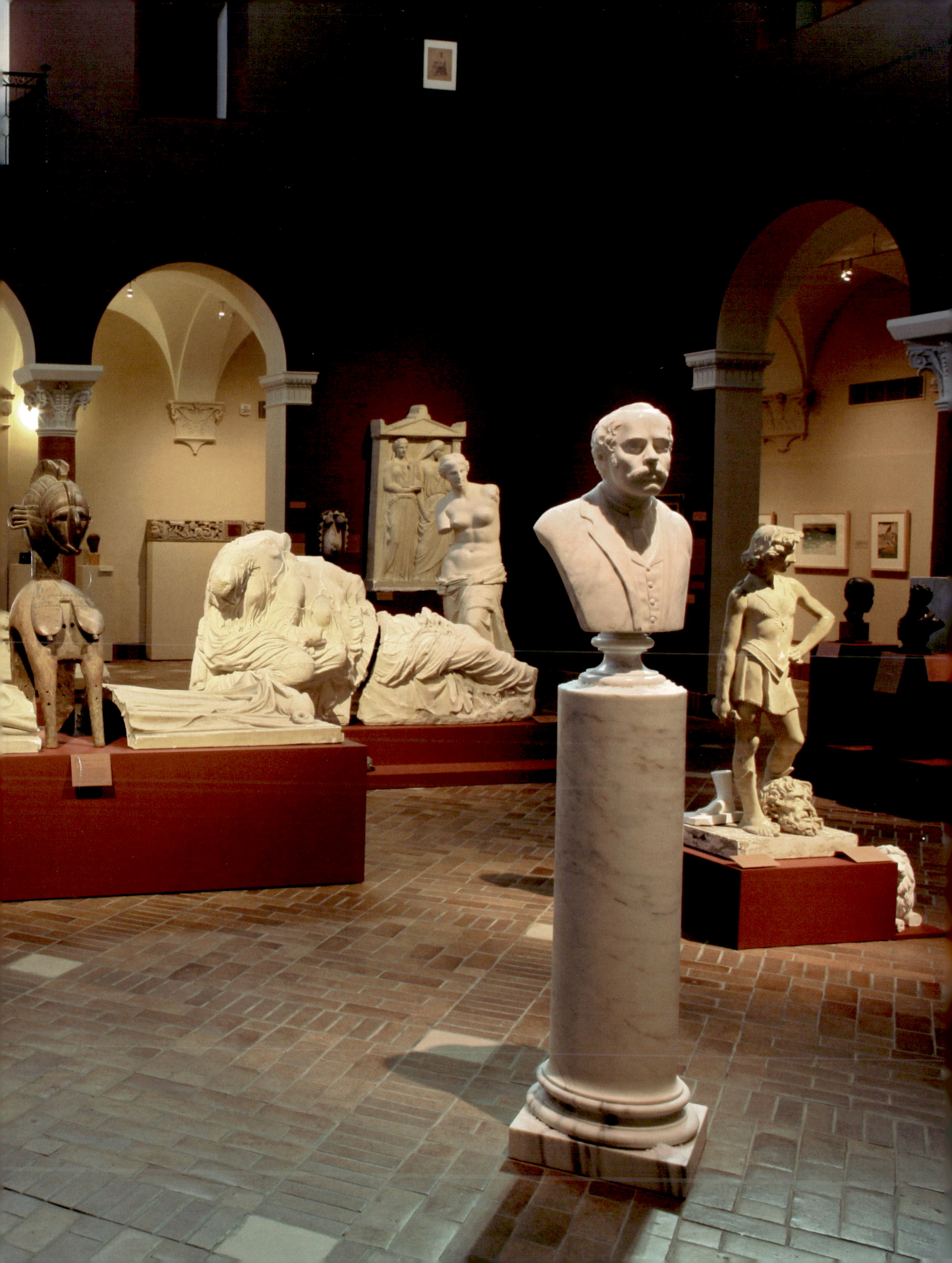

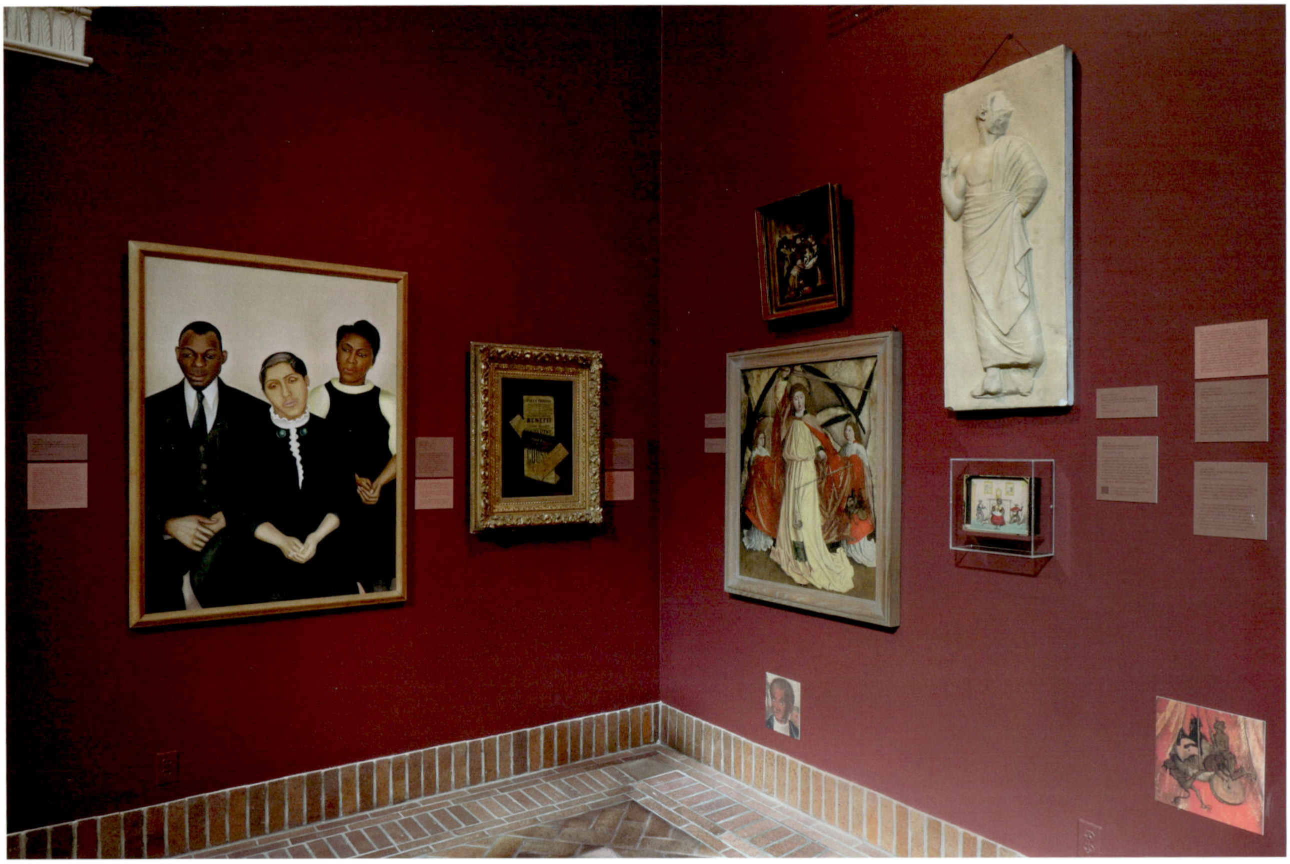

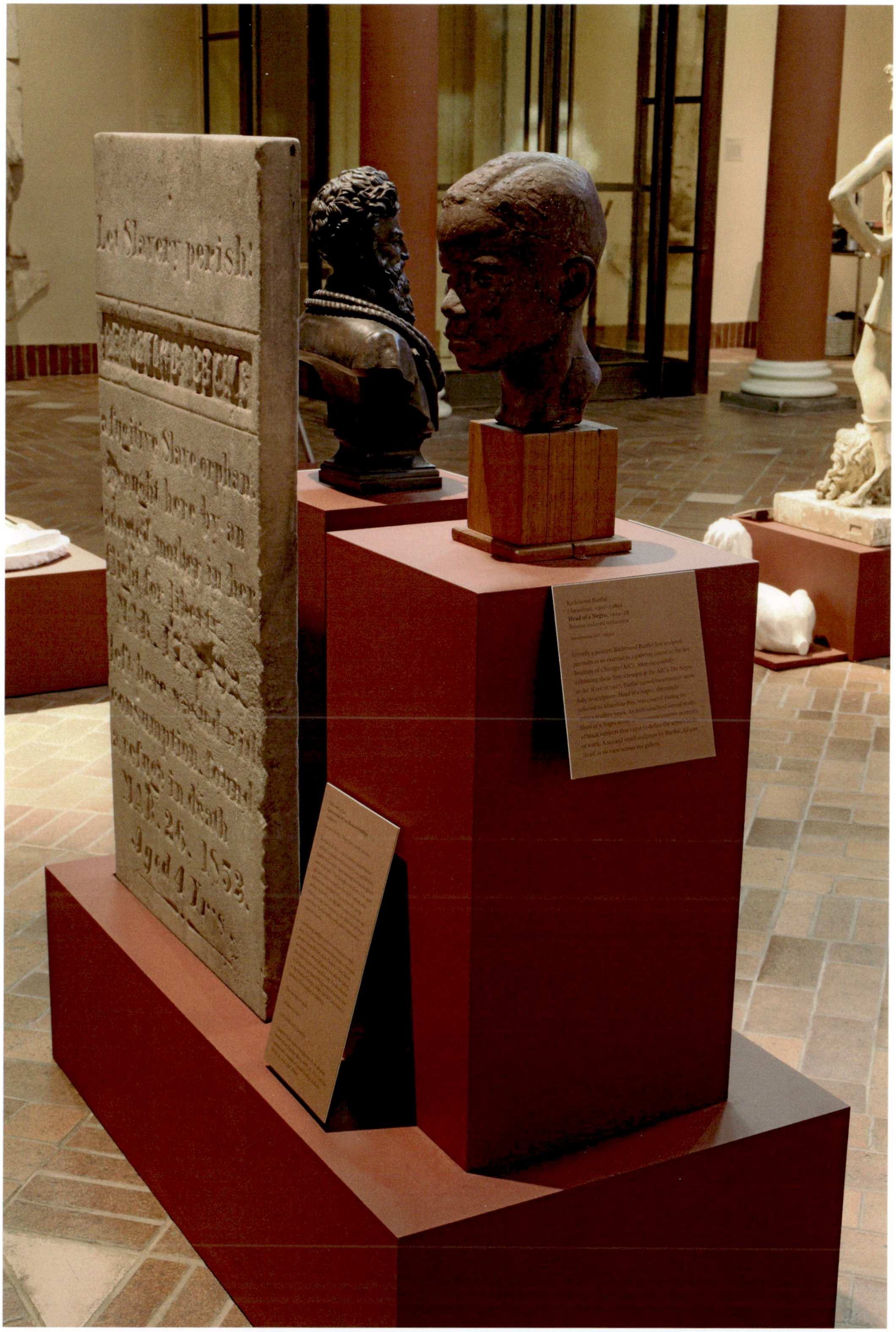
Let Slavery perish!
MAR. 25, 1852

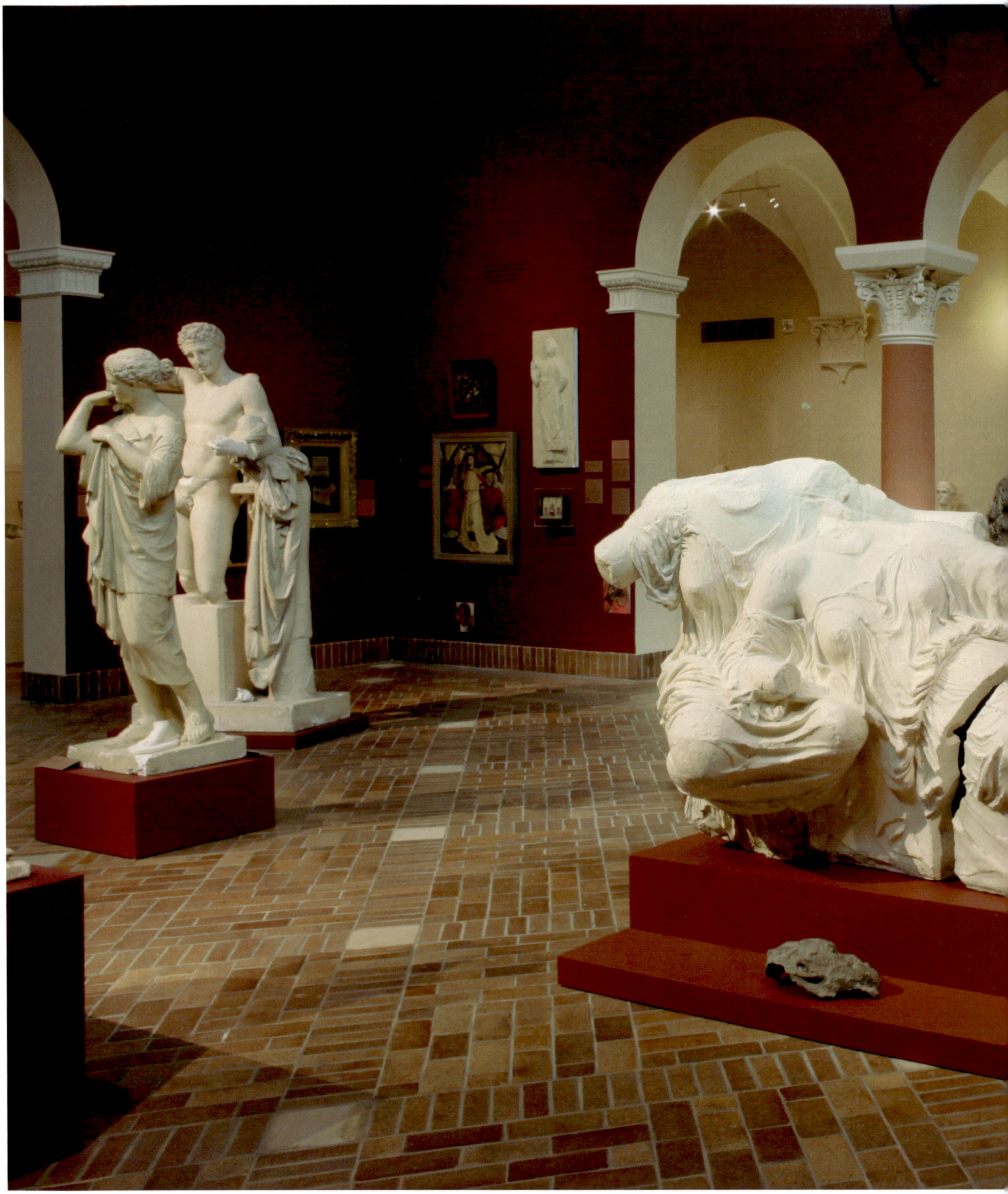

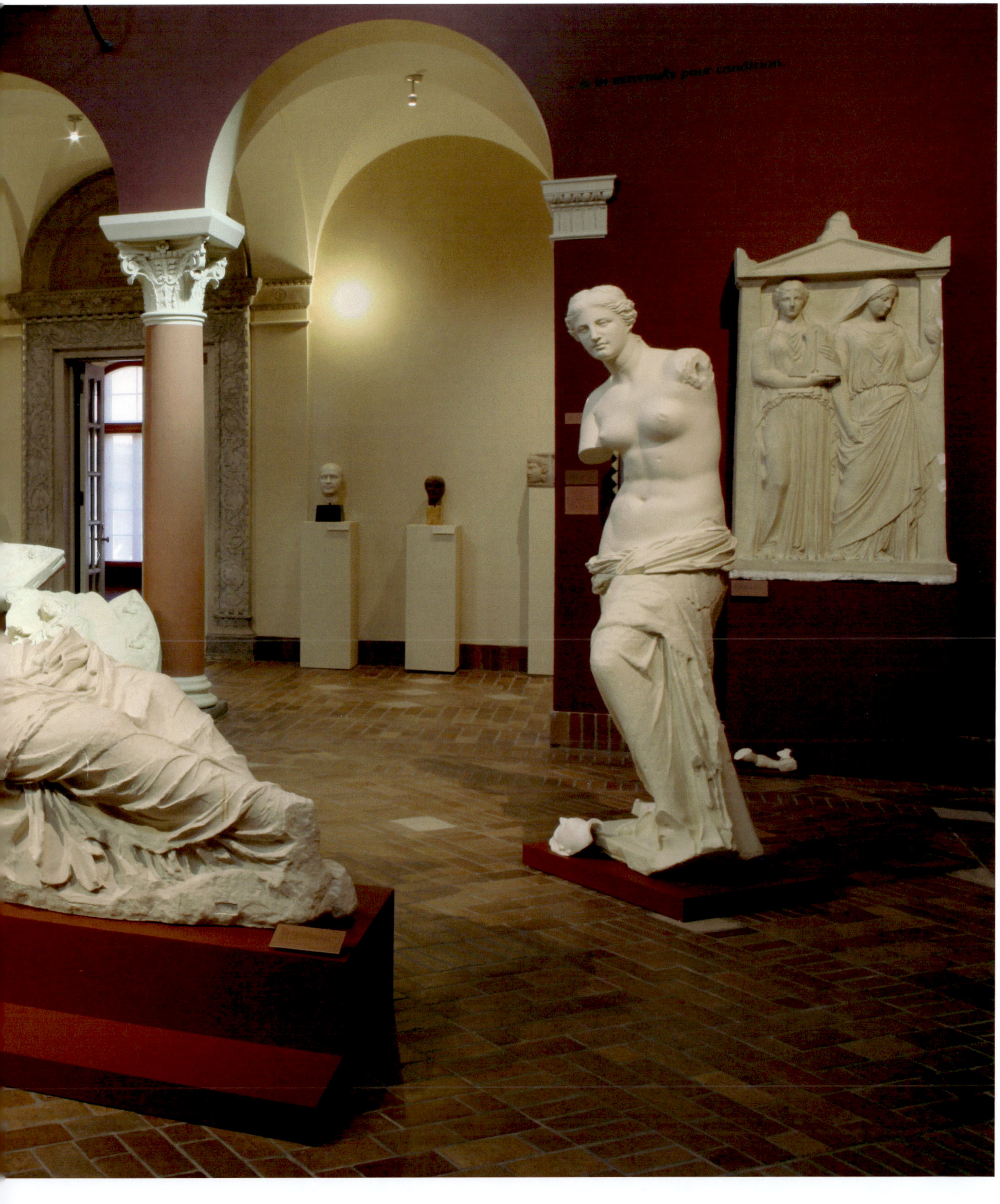

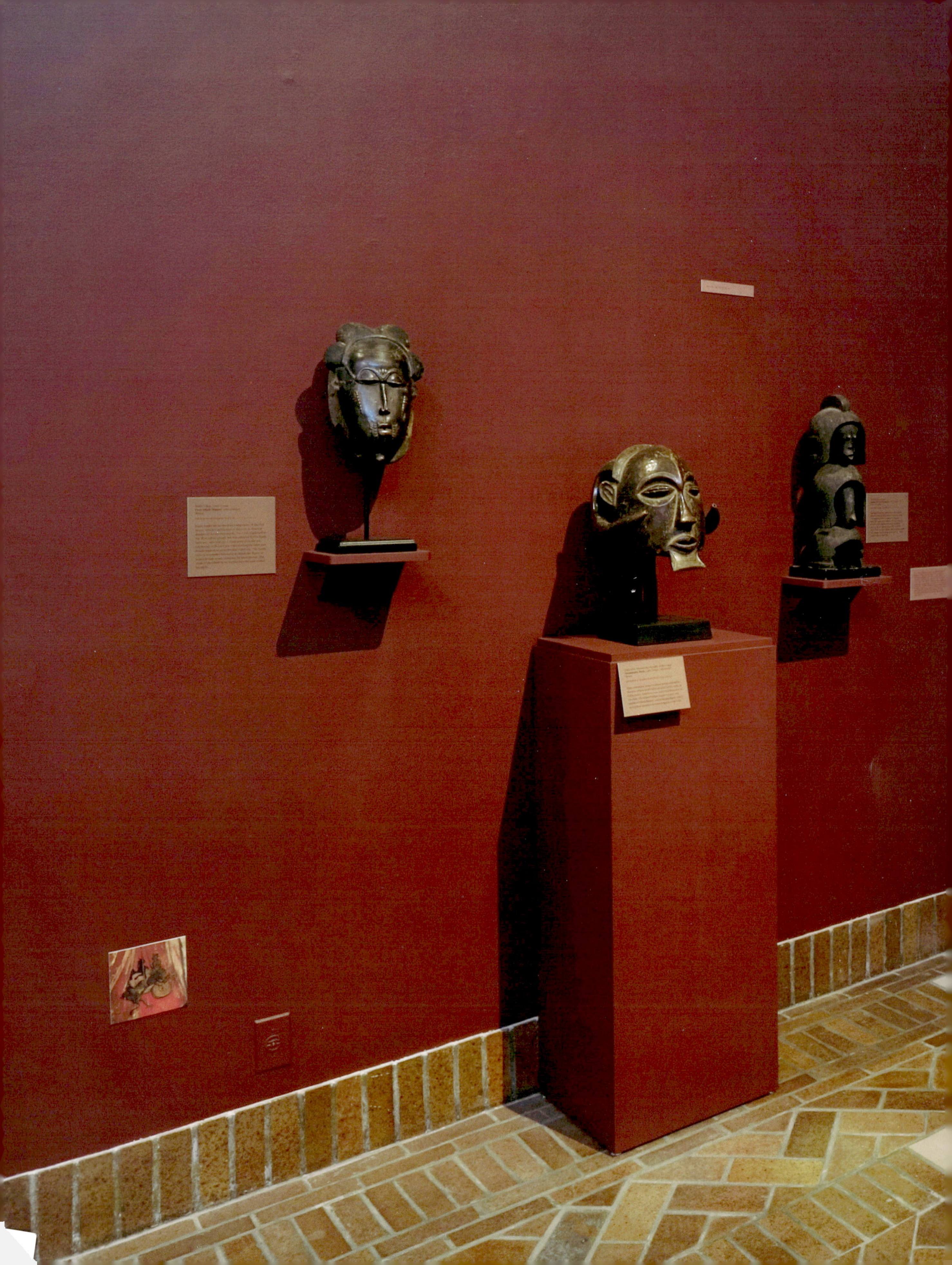

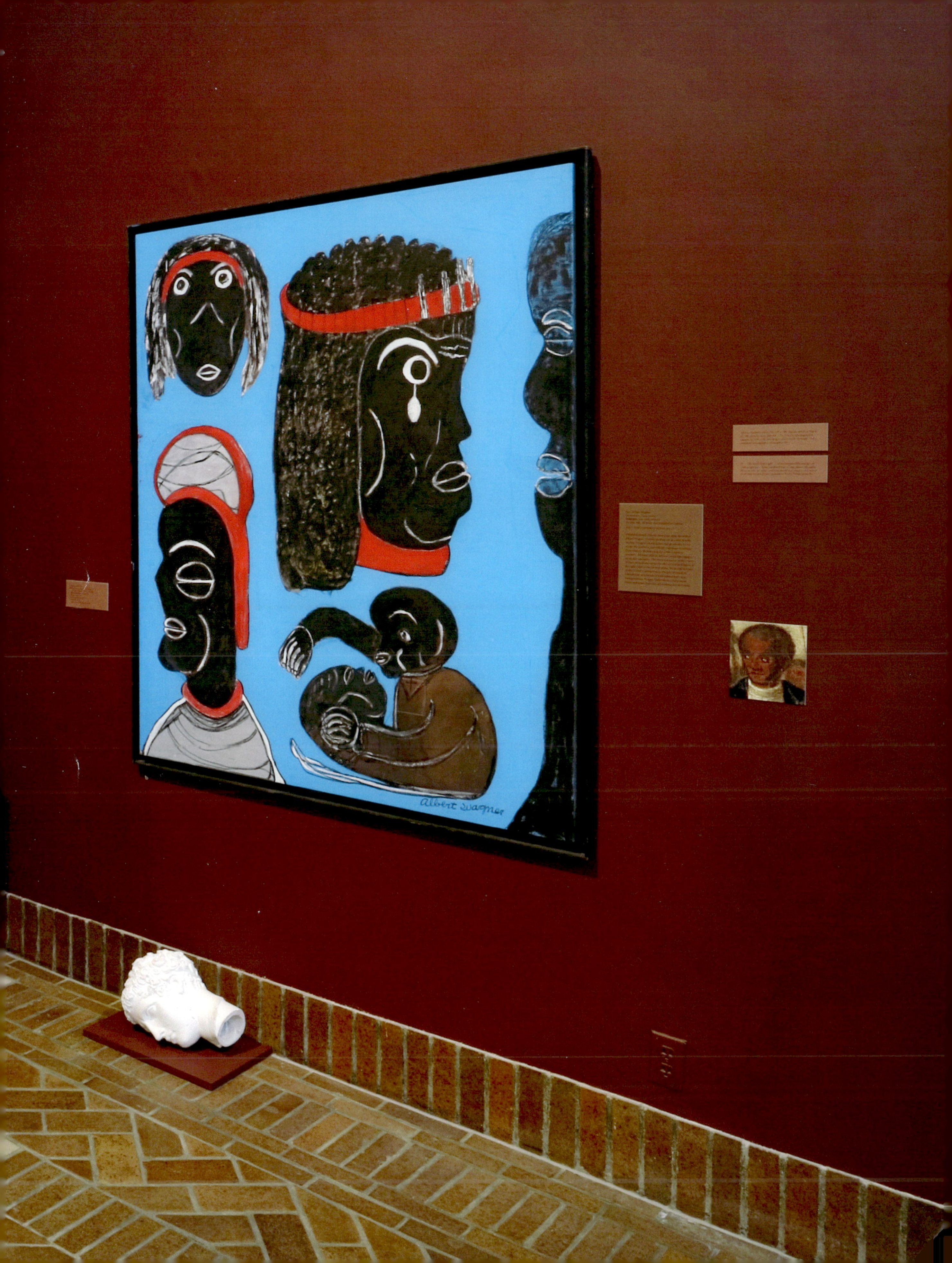
Albert Wagner

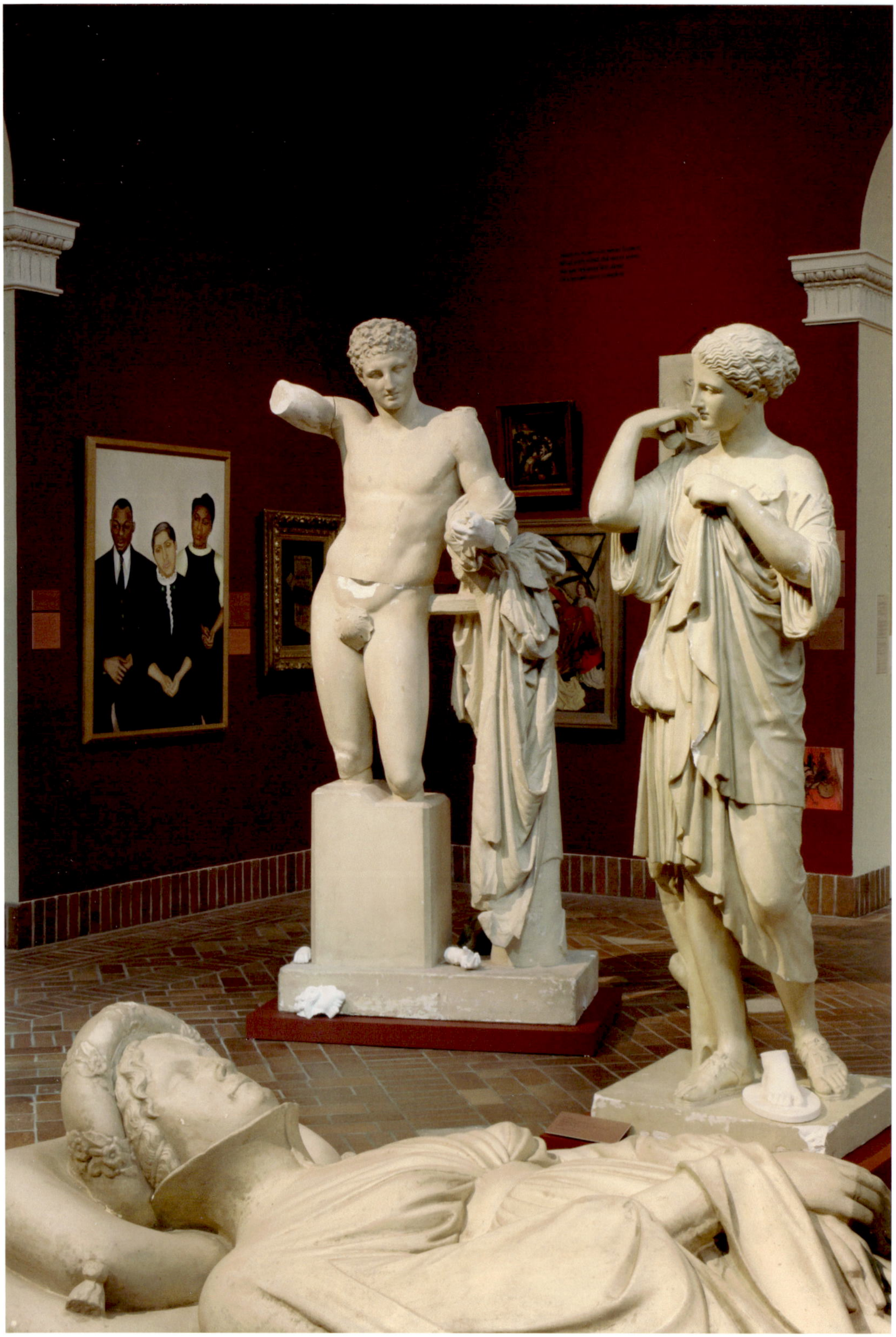

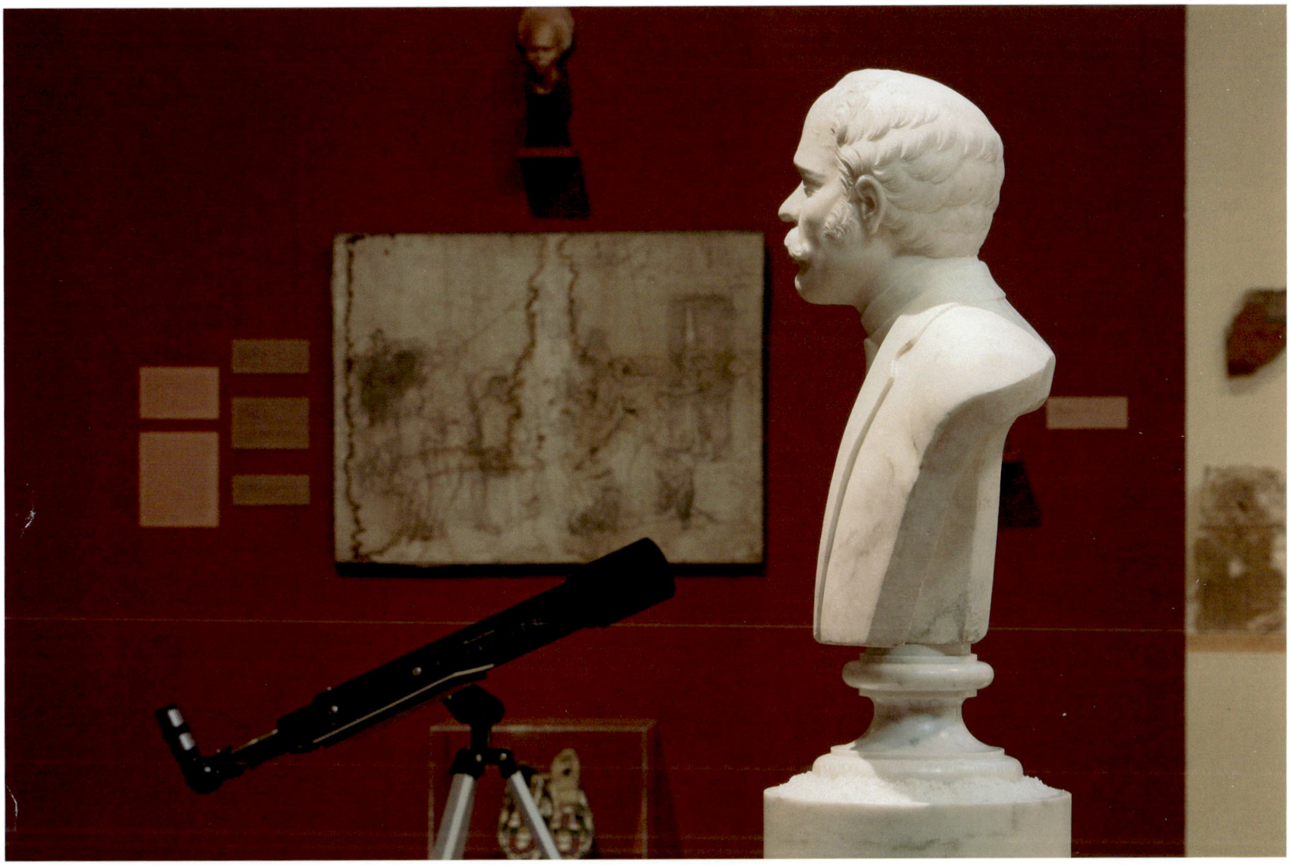

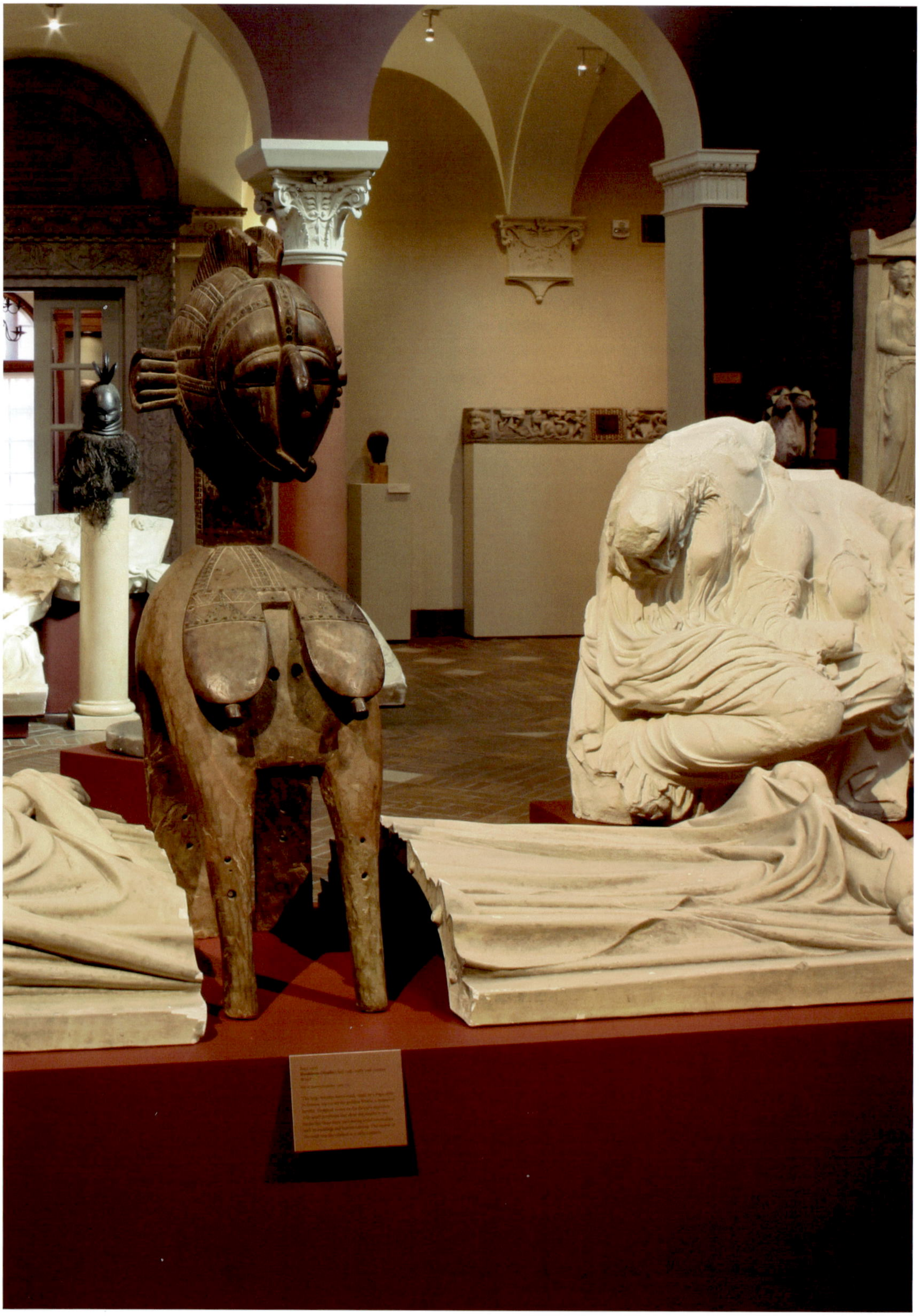

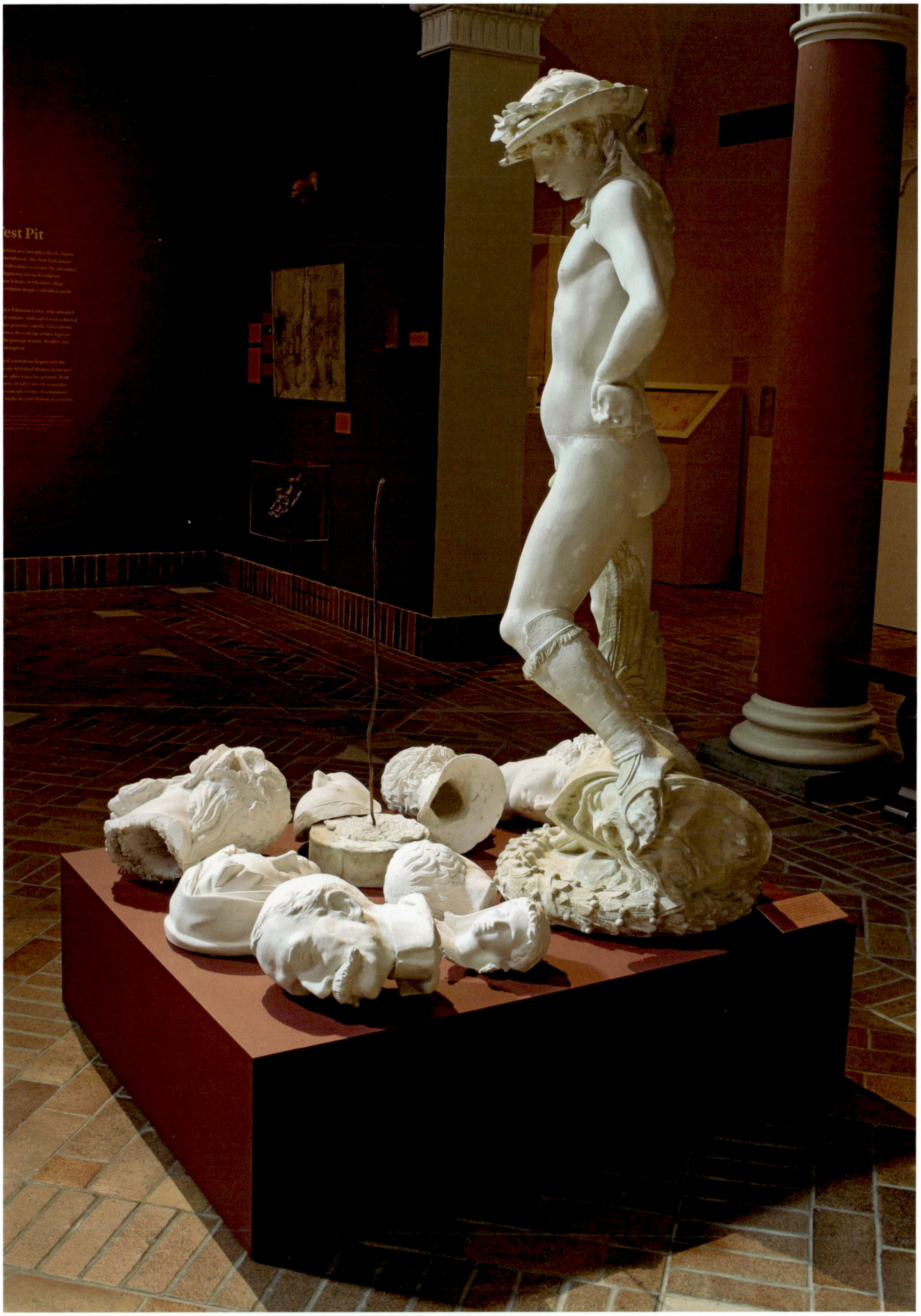

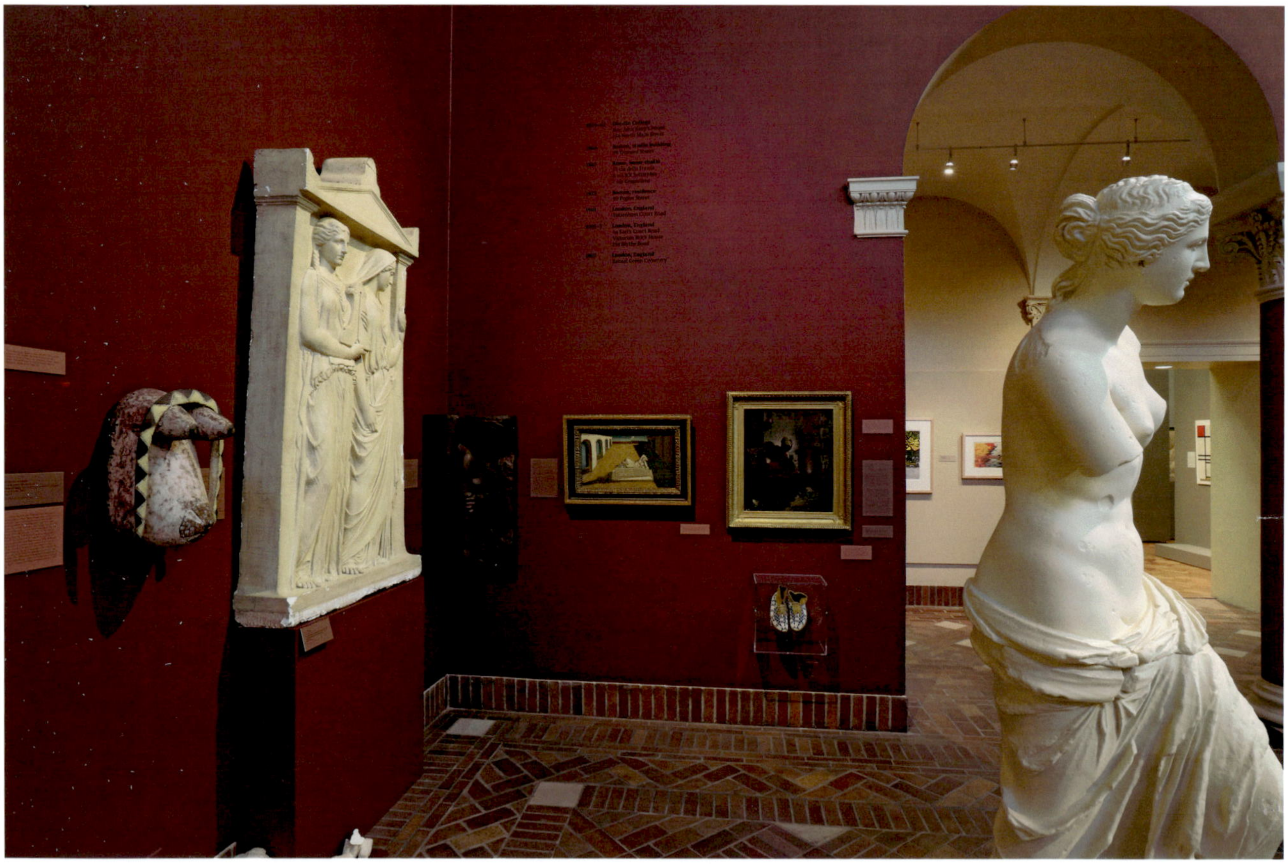

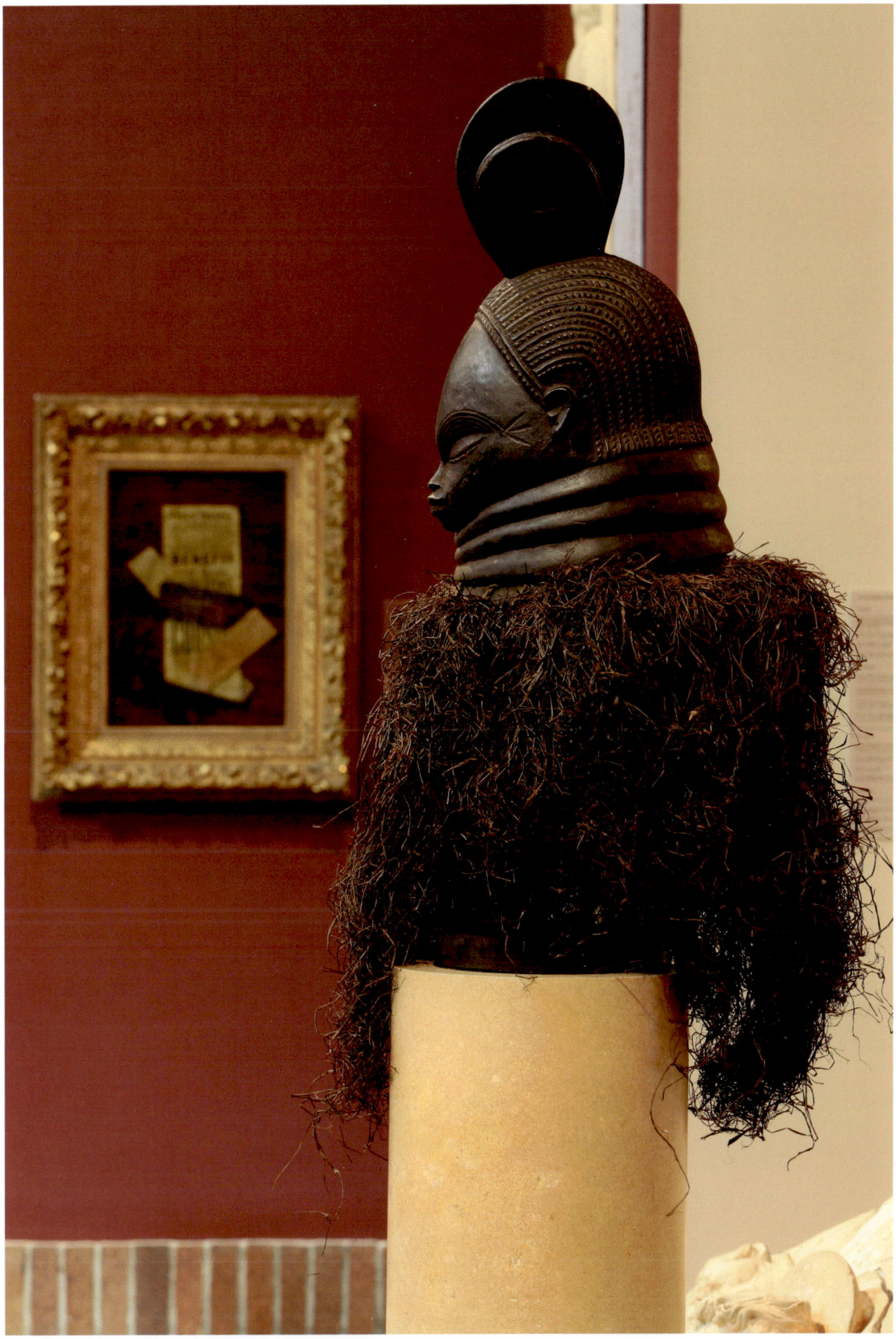

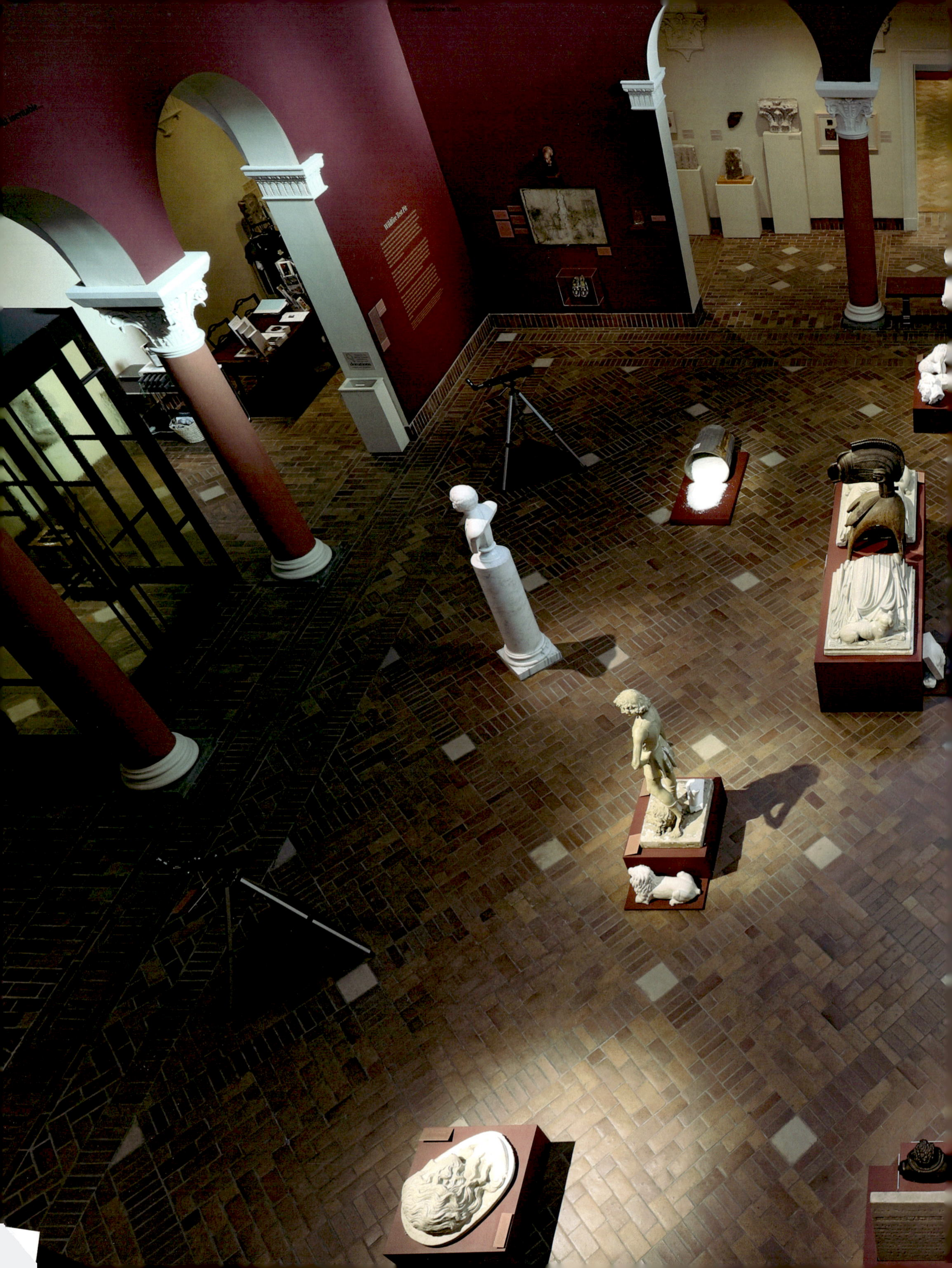
Wildfire Test Pit
donations

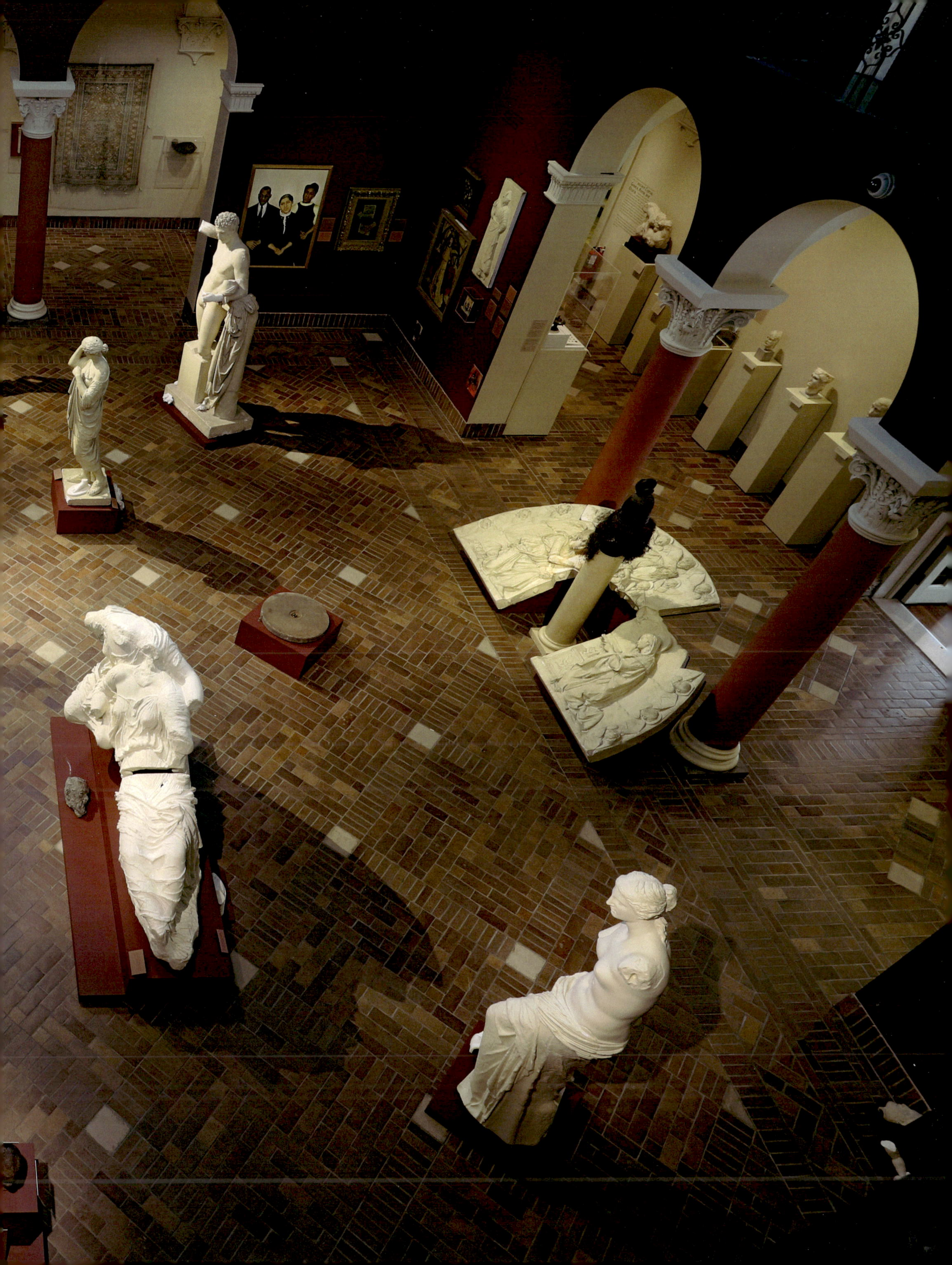

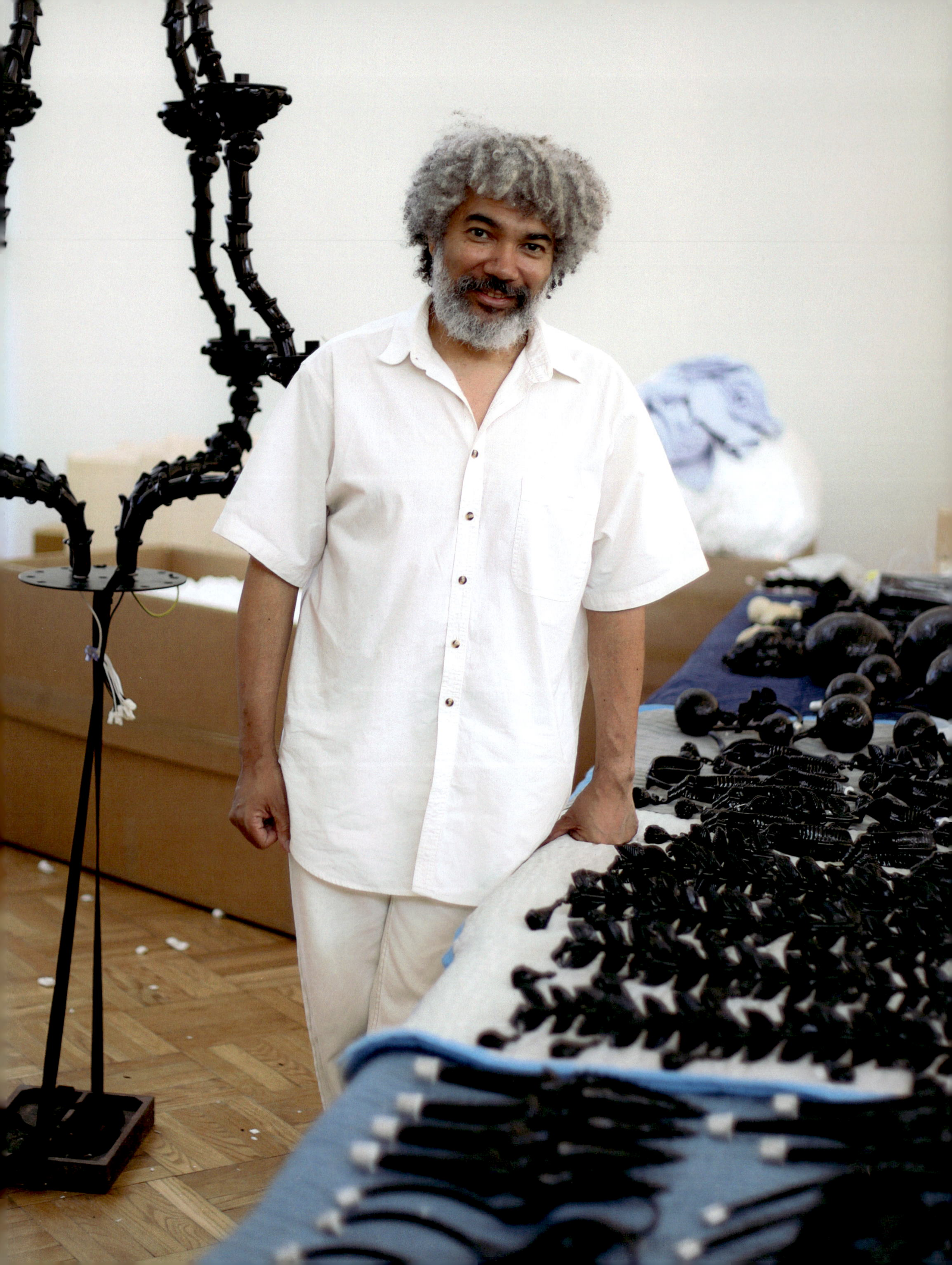

A Conversation with Fred Wilson

Andria Derstine

This conversation between Fred Wilson and Andria Derstine took place Saturday, August 27, 2016, at the Allen Memorial Art Museum as the finishing touches were being put on the exhibitions *Wildfire Test Pit* and *Fred Wilson: Black to the Powers of Ten.*

Andria Derstine Fred, thank you so much for speaking with me today about your exhibitions *Wildfire Test Pit* and *Fred Wilson: Black to the Powers of Ten.* My colleagues and I are thrilled to have worked with you on these projects, and that you have so thoughtfully engaged with the Allen Memorial Art Museum's—and Oberlin's—history, in the lead-up to the museum's centennial year. When you were first exploring the museum's collection in depth, in July 2015, what intrigued you?

Fred Wilson Hmm...I did see unusual things. When I first came, of course I didn't know what I was going to do, but just hearing about the plaster casts—and hearing that there were so many of them—I knew that I could do something no matter what. I just knew it. In the collection, I gravitated to things that were unusual. And I always wanted to see black subjects even though I didn't know if they were going to be germane. I had also known about Edmonia Lewis from previous visits, so I knew that was floating around, but I didn't know if that was going to be a thing. So I was looking at black subjects just to see what's there, and mostly I just note everything down that I see, that's interesting, even if I don't really know if they're going to go anywhere. And there were many things I saw that didn't go anywhere. But the painting by the Belgian painter, I forget her name now . . .

AD Angèle Watson.

FW Angèle Watson. I was attracted to her painting the moment I saw it (fig. 10). So, I didn't know if I was going to be able to put it in, but I just knew I liked that painting. And also, that little strange box.[1]

AD The mechanical box (page 36, center right).

FW It was something that I thought was fascinating, and of course is not emblematic of the collection at all, so it was really curious that it was there. I didn't know what to make of that. And there were other things that I didn't use, even though I really wanted to, because as the idea went down the pike, I couldn't, even though some juxtapositions were really interesting. For example, one was the dragon, and one was the figure that's leaning back . . .

AD Oh, the Rodin. The bronze Japanese dragon sculpture, and the Rodin.[2]

FW Yes, the Rodin. And they're in juxtaposition with each other, like they were both doing this [Wilson stretches his arms up in the air and looks up], they were euphoric, the two of them together and so I was trying to think, "I just really want to put this out there," but the project just did not go that direction.

AD It didn't go with the theme you were developing.

FW Yes. That was one compelling juxtaposition, but I couldn't use it. One interesting thing I remember, in storage with the museum's curator of

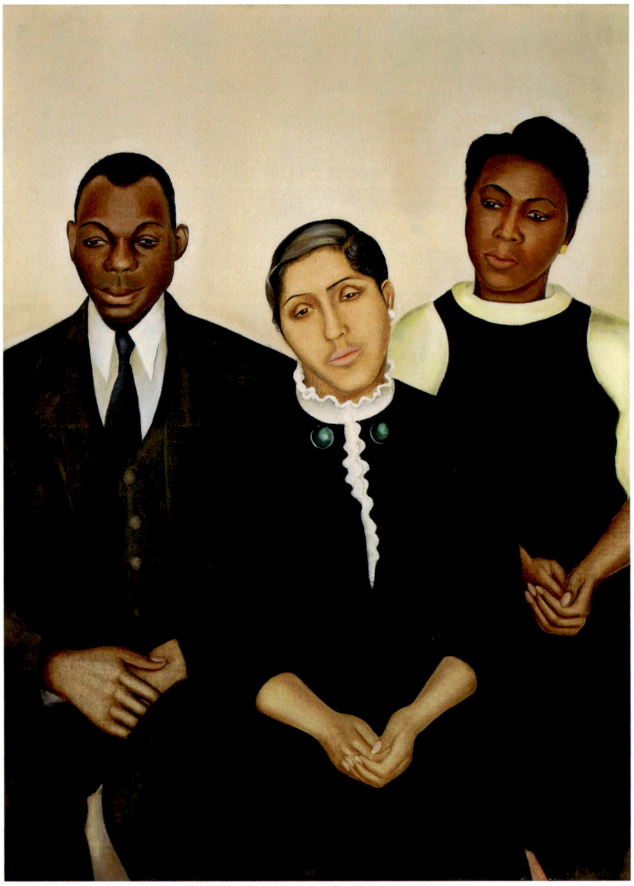

Figure 10. Angèle Watson (Belgian, 1886/87–1980), *Negro Family*, ca. 1930, oil on canvas. Anonymous Gift, 1938.24.

Asian art, was seeing the little display box for the Buddha (fig. 11). I immediately saw that. And it had resonance for me.

AD Right, because the sculpture itself was missing.[3]

FW The piece was sitting right next to it, but it was not in it. It just really resonated with me, because of what I've been thinking about in the past year, with what's going on in the Middle East. And then it just sort of broadened out from there, and again I didn't know if it was going to go anywhere but it was something I really liked. On view in the gallery was *The Present*, which I thought was a wonderful painting (page 15).[4] And so I needed to see, by also looking at works in storage, if this was a one-off kind of subject or if there was anything that could really be interesting with it—and again I didn't know where it was going, but Edmonia Lewis was in my head. You know, actually one of the other things I liked that wasn't in storage were the big paintings that were in the gallery . . .

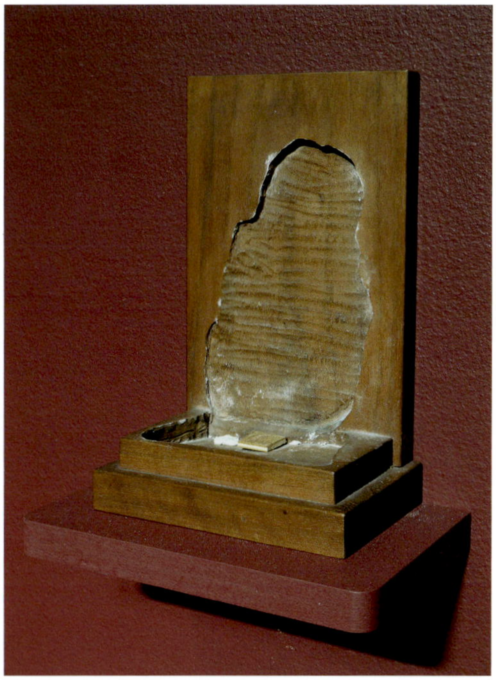

Figure 11. Base for Afghan *Seated Buddha* (5th century, R.T. Miller Jr. Fund, 1946.25), wood, 20th century.

AD The Thomas Lawrence paintings?[5]

FW Yes. And I was interested in the history of Thomas Lawrence, and India, but it wasn't going to fit. [chuckle]

AD Yes, there's that whole trade route aspect to that story, and their marriage—but it just didn't end up going with the rest of your theme.

You came here in July 2015 to work on this project in earnest, but you had visited prior to that, in February 2013, and back in September 2001. Prior to starting on this project, how much were you aware of Oberlin's—both the college's and the town's—progressive history? For example, the town's involvement in the Underground Railroad and abolitionism, and the college's admission of male and female students of all races? And how might that have played into your decisions about the exhibition?

FW I don't think I knew much, because when I first came, when Sharon Patton was the director, my visit was really brief. When I came back with Douglas Baxter,[6] in 2013, he must have filled me in a little bit on that because he was giving me the grand tour of Oberlin. So, he may have mentioned some of that stuff. Hindsight is hard for me, because now I can't get it out of my head. But, it might have been just Douglas giving me a tour with a broad brush.

AD And what would you say was the process by which you really came to focus on Edmonia Lewis, whose life is the guiding spirit behind *Wildfire Test Pit*, and her time at Oberlin and beyond?

FW Well, I'd always known about her. And, I think she's an intriguing, enigmatic figure in art history. And so I thought, "Well, this is just very serendipitous that she was here." It seemed like a perfect way to enter into it. And, I was trying *not* to say [in coming up with the theme of the exhibition], "Alright, this is it." I was trying to say to myself, "Well, *maybe*...and I'll just stop to look at her, and then I'll look around . . . and then I'd find myself looking back at her life—again. I kept looking at her." [laughter] Because I thought, "Is this an obvious choice? It's probably really obvious." But I just, eventually, found it really fascinating. And so unusual.

AD It is. And at least at Oberlin, certainly no one has focused on her recently in this manner, in this depth, I don't think. So it's new for all of us.

FW I did not know so much to start, but the more I asked [Oberlin College] people, and I spoke to them about what I was doing—the stories of what happened here in Oberlin became more and more fleshed out. And, I just wanted to know more.

AD And in addition to Edmonia Lewis, the museum's plaster cast collection is an important part of the exhibition, and the museum's history—and a collection that clearly resonates with your practice. How did the cast collection influence your thinking about the exhibition?

FW I would say, Edmonia Lewis was one guiding light, and the casts were the other. Because they possessed everything that she possessed in my thinking. The casts were embedded with nineteenth-century ideals that through time have taken a back seat to contemporary subjects and values. Their disappearance from view at the Allen was a telltale sign. This paralleled Lewis's disappearance; both she and her work had been forgotten, save the interest of a few scholars, until very recently. Even the casts that remained on the campus were considered unimportant. Some were unceremoniously stored in the library among the stacks, and were damaged and dirty. One was even comically and casually festooned with a tee shirt. There were many parallels that I could not ignore. Both Oberlin and the world had, at times, treated both the casts and what they represented, and Edmonia Lewis and her work, with disdain and indifference. I felt also that all these histories were unfinished . . . I loved the fact that Lewis was a presence. And, the fact that she's so enigmatic. You know, you have one sculpture by her and so much is out there—but "things not here" does not an exhibition make. So I liked the fact that there were casts here. I liked that there are pictures of them in the King Sculpture Court at one time. I liked the fact that, "where are they?" Well, they're not anywhere.

AD That's right.

FW I also liked the fact that some were here, but just hiding in plain sight.

AD Yes. Like at the library.[7]

FW So, I really do like things that are just not spoken, that are in your world but you really just don't notice them because they are just so much a part of your world and you don't think about them. Those are the things that intrigue me. Why, and how, and so the fact that she was a nineteenth-century sculptor, a neoclassical sculptor . . . you had these objects—they just dovetailed.

AD They went together and they started to tell a story.

FW And the fact they were, you know, in disrepair was really important. If they had been hallowed objects they might not have interested me as much.

AD And we are so happy that they did interest you; you've given new life to these works that were part of the earliest installations in the museum, almost a century ago.

On another subject, collaboration with other organizations has long been a hallmark of the museum, and it's exciting for us that you worked with many institutions beyond the museum, including the Oberlin Heritage Center and other campus collections. Beyond the Allen Memorial Art Museum, the college has materials that you've incorporated into the installation, such as works from the Archives and the library's Special Collections, as well as works you've purchased from local businesses, casts on loan from a local sculptor, and the grindstone acquired via the Amherst Historical Society as well. How have these works from outside the collection informed your thinking about the direction of the exhibition? Were there any unexpected surprises in what you found in these other repositories that took your work in a new direction?

FW What was great was, with these things, there was a visual history available to support a moment in history, particularly the Special Collections objects. I could have done the exhibition without them, but they're ultimately really important to it because they provide an interesting context and history for that time. And, even if it's early, you can place Edmonia within her consciousness of what was going on . . .

AD What was going on in Oberlin in the nineteenth century—through works like the gravestone or the bust of John Brown . . .

FW Exactly. And, again, these objects were in Special Collections—you know, historic objects, not necessarily seen as art, or viewed for their visual importance. They are intellectually important, but not displayed to reveal an emotive quality or elicit an emotional response within the context of those collections. And so, I try to add that in the context of what I'm doing.

AD The drawing *Urania* (fig. 12), by Edmonia Lewis, is not part of the museum collection, but is in the Oberlin College Archives. Could you talk a little bit about that drawing, and how it is important to the display, especially given its location in the exhibition?

FW Yes. It's important because—more than the bust of James Peck Thomas—it was the connector between her and neoclassical . . . not even neoclassical art, ancient art.

AD Exactly.

FW And so, it was a direct connection, and it was done here. All these things start to dovetail, once you start to formulate a theme or a pattern; all the matrices start to work together. It's fantastic. It's a diminutive drawing she did as a student. It's not the most powerful drawing in the world but it places her here. It places her interest really early in these things, and it places these neoclassical casts—even though they weren't here at that time—it just makes the context all the more interesting. And the more you get into it, you understand that she went to Rome, and obviously this *Urania* sculpture was there in Rome as well.[8] So, it just . . . It really pulls the whole thing together. And I put it where I put it, A, because I didn't want people to look at it for aesthetic reasons necessarily. It's a touchstone for her and for us in this whole history. But B, it was also something that I could see as her guiding light, this early image that kind of connected her to her future history. Although it was unreachable at that time when she was here, and she didn't know where it was going to go, but there it was. So it was really for her a guiding light even if she didn't know it. So, I wanted it to be something like that that was not touchable necessarily, but there, in her consciousness, and in our consciousness that it was there. And so, the fact that it's Urania, it just made sense. It was important to have the drawing just barely there, you can look through a telescope and know it's far away from you but also really see it up close through the lens. And so, it makes you focus on it and think about it, when displayed in another way you wouldn't.

AD And Urania being the muse of astronomy, it makes so much sense that you worked with the telescopes.

FW That's right. I love when things fall into place like that.

AD And that really did.

FW It really did. But another thing, is that my grandmother's name is Urania—she was born in the nineteenth century—although she hated [chuckle] that name, she went with Irma instead, her middle name. But, it was like Edmonia was saying to me, "You gotta do this, you gotta do this project."

AD Following on that, and thinking about *Urania* and its placement, your work, it seems to me, is often both immersive and highly participatory, in that you ask viewers to think about deeply embedded assumptions and to join you in the process of discovery. In this exhibition, you've incorporated visitor participation through the use of telescopes and a wide range of textual material—some of it enigmatic on the surface—that visitors will read and decipher. Can you speak a bit about your incorporation of these elements and the importance to you of a non-static visitor experience?

FW I didn't really think about the visitor experience, especially with the telescopes. It was just something that I needed to do, and I just wanted to see that happen. And in order to really understand what I was thinking I had to do this. So, it wasn't something like some museums might do, to enhance the visitor experience... It just made sense for the work and hopefully for others.

AD And the other object that visitors will look at through a telescope, the gold Baule female figure (fig. 13)—what was your thinking behind that?

FW Well, I had the balcony and I love the balcony.[9] And I don't know when it hit me to do that, but I liked that it was a diminutive object. I liked that it was gold colored and that it was African, and it was female. And I wanted to focus on it. To me, it's like a spirit, it's like some kind of astral figure or object. And so, it's sort of a guide, again, a guide for Edmonia even though she may not... I mean,

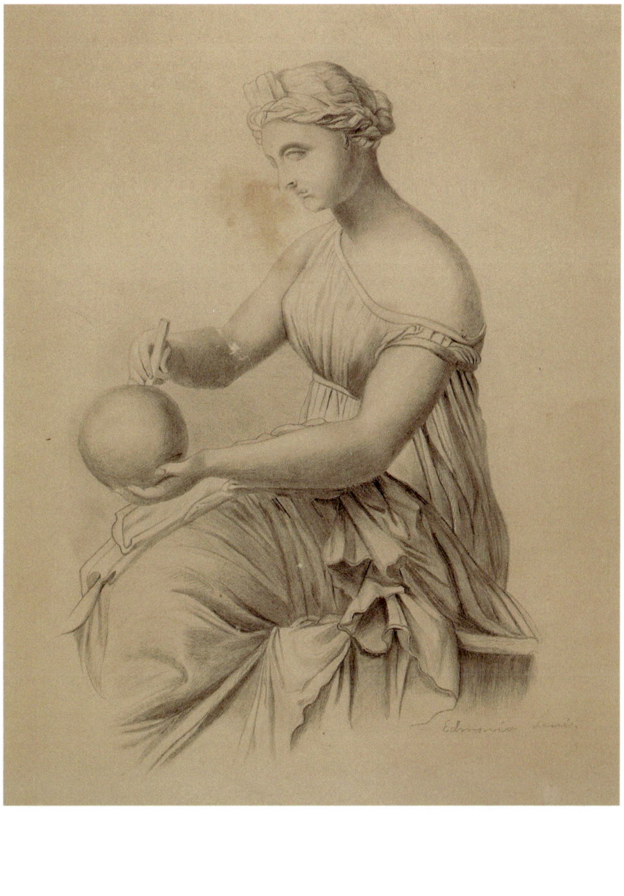

Figure 12. Edmonia Lewis (American, 1844–1907), *Untitled drawing after Urania, the Greek Muse of Astronomy*, 1862, pencil drawing on buff paper. Courtesy of the Oberlin College Archives.

she had no connection to Africa beyond the fact of her heritage. But, it's just sort of a guiding concept.

AD During the months of planning for the exhibitions, you spent time getting to know Oberlin College faculty from a range of disciplines including studio art, art history, history, Africana studies, anthropology, and other disciplines, and students. Are there any aspects of those meetings that impacted your work here at the museum or that helped you learn more about Oberlin past and present?

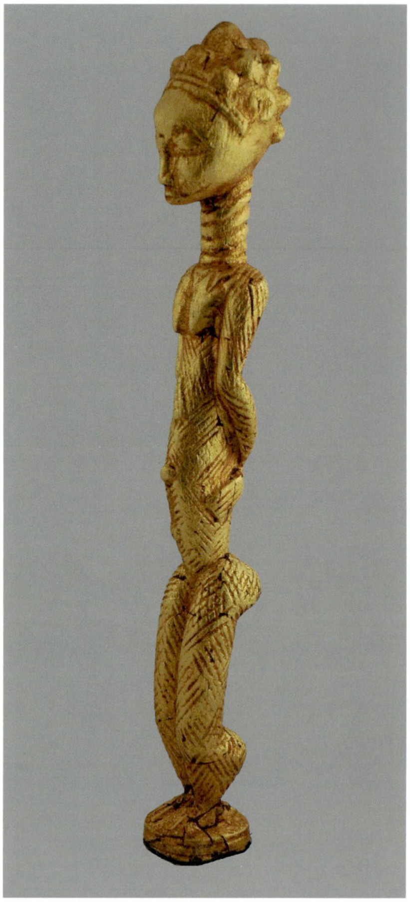

Figure 13. Baule artist, Ivory Coast, *Female Figure*, 20th century, wood and gold leaf. Gift in honor of Alexandra Gould (OC 2011), 2011.26.10.

FW Certainly, it was great meeting a whole lot of people, while I was just trying to understand the context within which this was going to be placed, and the kind of conversations that were going on here. It wasn't intended to be research, but it was. Because it was so early on, I wasn't hiding anything from anybody. But things that people said in those lunches and dinners or whatever we had, really informed the artwork. I did mention Edmonia Lewis, and several faculty had some thoughts about her and about what went on here—perhaps it was one of the first things that they talked to me about when I mentioned her, what happened here. And then also, the second thing was *Cleopatra* being here and what happened with that.[10] And so, that really intrigued me and, again, I wasn't sure that was going to enter into it, because it was a known story. Why should I just re-gild the lily? But, it was also clear that most people *didn't* know. I like placing even recent history within the work—not just ancient or historic subjects—and so, this brings it pretty close to now. So it all made sense as it went in the larger scheme of things; it stayed an important aspect of fitting into the whole work. So, yeah, I think it was about things the faculty had mentioned about Edmonia, but just generally just the campus—seeing and understanding a little bit more about the campus and also going to the...

AD The Mary Church Terrell symposium?[11]

FW Yes, it was also nice for me to do that, and it really made sense at that time.

AD It was terrific for the faculty and students to get to know you during this process. When I was a student myself, I was fortunate to be able to spend several summers working on an archaeological dig in Greece, and one of the things that's very meaningful to me about what you've done in this exhibition is the idea of a test pit. And I wonder if you could speak a little bit about that, about the archaeological aspect of the display. There are layers of works, and texts that visitors will see high up—and as they look elsewhere they'll see other types of artifacts.

FW Right. The space of the exhibition [the King Sculpture Court] literally is like a test pit for me, because it can feel as though you are inside of it. If you're upstairs [in the Ripin Gallery] you're looking down into it, but even when you're down in it, you feel like you're inside of something. I think painting the walls [deep red] makes it really feel like that.

AD Yes, it does.

FW Hindsight is 20/20—the texts and labels on the walls, it's like different strata of information. Some are big and bold, and some are small and diminutive. I want people to receive these things in different modalities, different speeds, and then eventually see how some of them relate. Because some people are not even going to see the things above, and some people are not going to read all those little notes... and you don't have to.

AD But it all works together if you choose to do that.

FW That's right. And I try to place the large texts far enough away from the artwork, because I wanted the artworks to still be artworks and not just...

AD Illustrations or something.

FW Yes. Or something that I'm using to a degree that you don't really think about, or where you wouldn't have a personal experience with the artworks. So I tried to keep the texts as far away as possible, but still have the relationship. That was really important. And the notes... I had wanted to use some images that I'd found but ultimately it didn't seem to make sense, or it seemed difficult, or I couldn't figure out how to use other images in the way that the notes work for me. And so, I decided—because I was doing all this research on Edmonia Lewis—I decided I wanted to just go directly to the footnotes... and, to me, it's a celebration of research.

AD It is.

FW The notes are like miniature metaphors, and the idea of a test pit is also like a miniature metaphor for footnotes, because people are constantly digging, and the deeper you dig, the more you learn and you review other people's work. . . How other people have been digging and what they've found, and the relationships. Meaning and knowledge come from all this... So much work has been done on a subject and you start with some information, but really not a lot. And then, all this constant dialogue between...

AD Between scholars.

FW Between scholars.

AD Or between artists, between intellectuals, between readers, between writers. I think it's a perfect metaphor for the educational institution where this is.

FW Yes. Well, and again, I would not have done it in a museum that was not in a college or university. I think that it's all about this place. It's all about that kind of research that is so incredible about colleges and universities. And there are really disembodied footnotes. It's not like I'm saying whose book this was. So it's really about this experience of the camaraderie of scholars, and sometimes they correspond, sometimes they say exactly opposite things, and sometimes it's because of the time period—new information is gotten, so the early ones are wrong date-wise or whatever. But the later ones correct it or fill in the gaps. And as I was doing all this, I know so many of these people—and particularly because the subject was Edmonia Lewis, many of them are African American scholars and there's even Romare Bearden, who's an artist. And of course, many women scholars talking to each other via their books and that really...I'm just thrilled with that. That's why I didn't put in the name of whose book it was who I was quoting, it's not about that, it's about this...

AD Inner dialogue among the scholars and among the readers and the writers.

FW Exactly, and I hope that comes through and it becomes very poetic in the snippets of information that the viewer has to put together in some way. And as a grouping, you gain some interesting knowledge but the relationship between my little odd footnotes and the images that are there, there are analogies, there are ironies, metaphors in the relationships between these things and it's working, for me, in the same ways that the paintings or artworks are working. It's not giving you everything on a platter. You have to understand, figure out the context, what's important about it.

AD Right. Bring your knowledge to it and learn something from it.

FW That's right. And as you go through, hopefully people gather more information and more knowledge about some of the relationships of this history and its importance, just from doing that. But others won't, they just may look at the artwork, which is fine too.

AD Which is fine too, exactly. And I think you've gotten to this somewhat, but I'll ask it anyway: there are so many layers of meaning in *Wildfire Test Pit*; what do you most hope visitors will take away from it—and maybe there's not just one answer to that.

FW No, no. Well, one thing is the fact that it's at a college. I hope that people, faculty and students, kind of "get" how to engage with this particular work. I imagine faculty will be bemused but also intrigued...

AD Yes. And that's partly our job, as a museum staff, to communicate that throughout the coming academic year. Not speaking for you, but helping them to understand your intentions.

FW Yeah. It's an exhibition but it's not *really* an exhibition... And they'll see themselves in their own research and their own fields, in it, but it's not about them or about a particular line of thinking. So I think I would not have done this if I wasn't here, at Oberlin.

AD And Oberlin has been fortunate to have your interest! I'm going to move on to the other exhibition, *Fred Wilson: Black to the Powers of Ten*. This is the first time that your studio-made or fabricated works have been displayed in an exhibition (*Black to the Powers of Ten*) at the same time and venue as one of your installations using a museum's permanent collection (*Wildfire Test Pit*). Did this pose any challenges for you? How do you feel that these exhibitions perhaps complement each other—being on view at the same time, at the same place?

FW Well, because at first, with what became *Wildfire Test Pit*, I didn't know what I was going to do, I had no idea whether they'd be complementary at all. However, it is me doing all of it [chuckle], so there are relationships, and I think *The Mete of the Muse* really demonstrates that. I was attracted to the figures, the plaster casts, because I am attracted to neoclassical and figurative art and sculpture. So that made sense for me and gave me an opportunity to do more of that in *Wildfire*. So I think there are overlaps in that way, and also in what I'd call cross-continent history, of African Americans and the diaspora, it's a continuum. But I really like the fact that they [the exhibitions] totally look nothing alike.

AD That's true, and I hadn't thought about it until now—even Edmonia, she crossed the ocean in the opposite way, to go to Italy—so there is a lot of interplay around the Atlantic, actually, with both of these exhibitions.

FW That's right.

AD And with all your work, it seems to me (and to others) that the past is present. While many of the works on view in *Black to the Powers of Ten* were created prior to some of the recent pressing problems facing the United States and, indeed, the world, today—I'm thinking about what has led to Black Lives Matter, for example, and the spate of shootings of people of color and other marginalized groups—the meanings of those works that you've done, even before this news has been hitting us, resonate very strongly at present. Can you speak a bit about how persistent issues of racism and discrimination, and perhaps problems such as the displacement of peoples, and economic inequality, have led you to create the works on view in that exhibition?

FW The works in that exhibition, because they were done over different periods of time, they tend to be about race, be about mourning, be about the history of things that are black. The resonance between *Wildfire Test Pit* and *Black to the Powers of Ten* is probably seen most strongly in the flags, because it's about the diaspora, but it's very different than *Test Pit*... Because I was interested in the history of flags and what they meant for black people wherever they were when they were creating their countries, after colonialism, and what color means, and meant when they were created. And so I think that is the overarching theme—not specific to the American theme right now, but it's an overarching theme. And so *The People*, that painting, is very specific in that, looking at the symbols and all the color black, looking at not only the African diaspora, but even the South Pacific (fig. 14). In the flags that the black symbols in this painting come from, the black symbols represent "the people". I found great personal empowerment from this notion that the flags themselves project pride, and empowerment is projected internationally—acknowledging this as a huge difference from the past.

AD Right.

FW I'm trying to think what other things are like that. Well, the drips. Because I'm interested in the color black and how it overlaps with things. The drips always look like oil or tar. Or ink, to me. Some people call them "tears", which is fine with me. I like to look at all those histories and how they interlace with world history. I have a work that's not in the show titled *The Unnatural Movement of Blackness*; a globe that is a mapping of the Atlantic slave trade and the Indian Ocean slave trade, and it also is a mapping of the consumers and producers of oil; all made with black chandelier parts. And so, it's a mapping of the corrupt economy of slavery in the nineteenth century, and oil, the corrupting economy of the twentieth...

AD Of the twentieth and twenty-first...

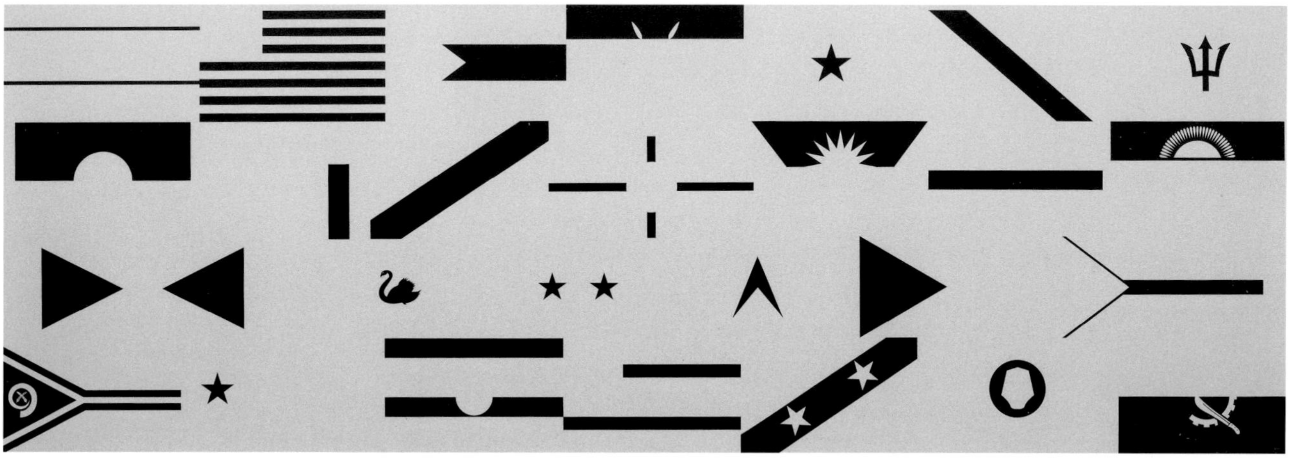

Figure 14. Fred Wilson (American, born 1954). *The People*, 2010, acrylic on canvas. Courtesy of the artist.

FW And so in that way, there is a relationship, certainly, with the nineteenth century with these ideas coming, and connecting...

AD Right, connecting to the present. And in these works and others, your practice seems to be imbued with collaborations—certainly in your installations, but also in your fabricated art. Your work with glassblowers and printers, for example, is highly collaborative by nature. To what extent does work with others feed your practice?

FW I went to art school like everybody else, and I used to make things. I do less and less of that, almost none. I juxtapose things.

AD Well, you have ideas.

FW I know, I'm working in a different mode... and in order to do these things, it's been really fruitful, satisfying for me, when I work with people who make specific things—artisans or craftsmen or people who work with specific materials—and that I know them to a degree, that I know what they make before I've met them. And so, it's kind of like what I come up with is something that they intrinsically know how to make. They've never made it before, it's nothing they *would* make, but they are forms that they feel comfortable making. So my ideas are coming through their hands. And so—and this is a difficult thing—if those particular people decide "We're not doing it anymore", I would stop making those things.

AD Right. It's great because of that collaboration between you.

FW That's right, and they enjoy these other ideas. And it's not something that they wouldn't make. I've talked to some of my glassblowers, like the famed Dante Marioni, and Janusz Posniak...They can make anything in blown glass.

They can make it, but if they don't feel it, it takes them longer to figure out how to make it to my desired form because it is not a form that they would create naturally. But they really understand and enjoy making my forms, and their work is spectacular. We really enjoy and respect one another, but our creative methods are absolutely opposite. So really, everything in that show is fabricated by somebody. The paintings as well. My studio assistant, Jason Irwin, makes the paintings. And the only reason I came up with those images, that way of making the image, is because that's what he was really good at. He was good at making this kind of technique. And it's difficult to do, but he's very comfortable making it, and it's satisfying for him. And it's the same with the glassblowers, and it will be that way into the future, for me.

AD I want to circle back to something you mentioned earlier. We were talking about the drips and the oil and the ink that we see in them now. And you also mentioned the fact that some people call them tears and that you don't mind that—but we know that you call them drips. I'm wondering if you can remember, back to, shall we say, the Ur-genesis of them, were you already thinking about oil or ink? You certainly weren't thinking about tears, because you said other people brought that interpretation to them. What led to them—was it just the beauty of the form, the gravity of the form of the glass? What were you originally thinking?

FW I went to this glass school [Pilchuck Glass School], not knowing what I would make in glass—but I was going to find out. And prior to that I had been making ink spot drawings, and they never satisfied me. I never liked them, and so I have never shown them. I didn't like how it looked, basically. It wasn't very satisfying as an image. So that was, for me it was a natural progression with glass—to come up with that form. Along the way, before I came up with the form, I actually tried dripping glass, to see what that would do, and that was... It didn't go anywhere, but it was something I had to try to do.

AD It was a step in the process, though, that led you to the drips.

FW Right. And so the drips became an object, rather than an image as a result of a process. At Pilchuck, I worked with Dante Marioni, and had him make a form that looked like a huge drip. This form, it looked so much like a drip that I continued... I always called them operatic. Renée Fleming, the opera singer, came to one of my openings, and I told her that I felt the drips, tears in this case, were "operatic." And I don't know if she understood what the hell I was talking about, because I didn't get a chance to go into it... But they're larger than life. And they're full of emotion, and they're intensely beautiful. So to me it's like that. I realize that they're over the top in a certain way, but I like that a lot.

AD And they kind of start small and then grow to a crescendo.

FW That's right. Yes, that's true. Yes.

AD And the shininess of them is also very attractive, as you said.

FW Right. And they're different, like notes; they're different and they change. And they combine in different ways, and so they seem to bring out different "arias". I think opera is a good connector, because there's tragedy, there's beauty, there are all these things that are very similar to how I feel about the drips. However, *Whether or Not,* the large drip work in the show, is operatic in scale, but it feels to me more related to precipitation than anything else I've done with the drip form. I think it holds up well to the other works in the show, which I feel was installed beautifully, by the way.

AD Thank you; the museum staff really enjoyed working with you on that. Changing the subject a bit, while very cohesive, in terms of theme, your work encompasses many different media. In *Black to the Powers of Ten*, visitors will see sculpture, painting, glass, prints, and video, as well as works that deal with past museum installation practices—I'm thinking particularly about *Black Memory* and *Black Present* (fig. 15). Can you speak about how you come to determine the medium that will be appropriate for your ideas?

FW It's the other way around, I think. Well, with the drips, it *is* true. I started doing drops on paper, because I wanted to sort of animate this very inanimate material, and relate it to childhood memories of stereotypes, of cartoons of black people as inanimate materials like ink or tar or things like that. But it had to have some gravitas, not just be an illustration of that idea. And so I sort of backed into glass. One of the glass people at Pilchuck, actually, Dante Marioni's father, Paul Marioni, said to me, as we were working, "The first one's free!" And I'm like, "What do you mean? I'm never going to do this again." [laughter] That was in 2001.

AD Right. And now look at you—glass is a big part of your work.

FW But I'll work with it until I've exhausted interesting ways to deal with it, then I'll move on to something else. And the mirrors and the chandeliers—because I was so heavily invested in Venice, and thinking about the affluence of Venice, which I had thought of for many years before I did the Biennale—spending that year working on it, it just... It became really important. And using *Othello*, taking it apart and using parts of the story... It wasn't a guide, it's a way to enter into the work that has many other subjects, but it's a way to enter into it. I use early Venetian design, and so it enabled me to bring up some personal things through this other form, and no one would know that they're personal to me. Basically it was a way to enter into it and see it not just as a chandelier, but as something else, and having another kind of meaning. And *Othello* is a tragedy, both play and opera, that always gets me. I've watched them all [all the versions], and I get upset every time.

AD It's terrible. You've seen it so many times, and it still hits you in the gut, what happens there...

Your work, dealing as it does with such topics as memory and time, the latter of which is our museum theme this year, can be considered in some sense nostalgic or elegiac. How did you come to your great interest in history and in received historical narratives? And maybe you could speak a little bit about your interest in history as a younger person.

FW Fascinating. I really don't know where this came from. It was not particularly my interest. However, I have to say a couple of different things. When I got out of art school, the world was really different, and the art world was really different. And there was no way in New York City that I was going to—within the mainstream—was I going to be a part of it. They just did not see African Americans as a part of it. And of course, in college they never told you that. In fact, the dean of the art school did, the year I was leaving, say to me, "Are you going to be part of the black art world or the white art world?" And...

AD Wow.

Figure 15. Fred Wilson (American, born 1954). *Black Present* (detail of interior), 2006, ink wells, oil cans, and resin skeleton installed in wood and glass vitrine. Courtesy of the artist.

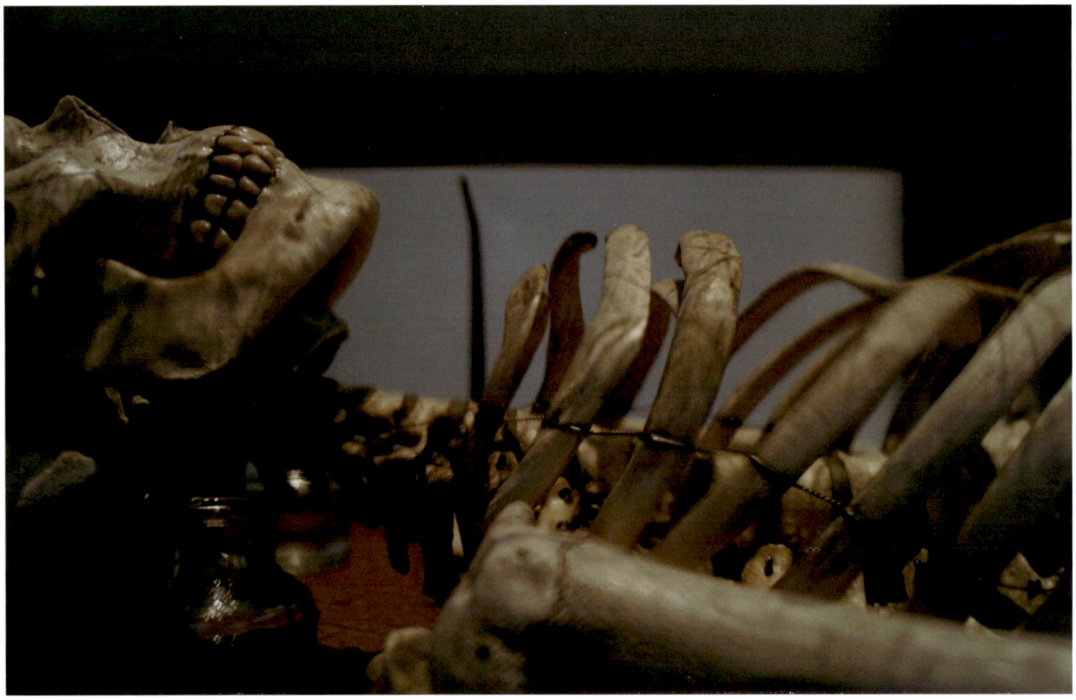

FW I thought to myself, "All these years, you never told me there was this [difference]..." So, basically, it was like, do you want to be visible, or do you want to be totally invisible and make no money and blah, blah, blah. I didn't realize that it was like this, and there it was. And it wasn't because black people were, you know, trying to have it like that. And then he didn't explain any more about it. And so the unspoken was, "Alright, out you go into the world."

AD "Good luck!"

FW Yeah. And then there were other experiences that I don't have to go into, that made clear that this was true. And, you know, there wasn't this kind of "everything for art, everyone for art." So, where did we start out with this question? I want to answer it.

AD About your interest in history.

FW Oh. So, that was a shock to the system. It was such a shock because I was the only black student in the art school at that time. And then coming to New York City and not even knowing all the black artists that were here, because nobody ever said anything about them, or even the historic figures. So I just felt like it was a complete snow job, and a complete elitist kind of environment. And so I felt very betrayed, not because of the situation it was, but because no one ever said anything about it.

AD No one ever explained it or talked with you about it.

FW No. And so I retreated to... Well I didn't retreat. I basically decided that I wanted to work with real people. And so, I got a job in East Harlem working with teenagers and children and senior citizens. I ran art programs, was a director for art programs for a social service agency. And I also taught at the Met[ropolitan Museum of Art], or taught classes outside the Met for the Met. And because I'd already been to Africa by then, I taught about African art and that sort of thing. So I just really retreated... And I knew I was going to make artwork, but I just didn't worry about the art world. And so, I think because of this. . . it kind of made me start looking deeper and looking at all the incongruities and all these things that now we're talking about. And going to museums through that lens, seeing how they were not talking to me or anybody like me. Talking as if I was invisible—and so reading the labels, seeing the environment of the spaces, it kind of got me really upset. Even, say, at the Peabody Museum at Harvard, talking about indigenous people as if no one else other than white people were going to read these things. And the biases just jumped out at me in all these kinds of museums, and the museums were just clueless about it, because they're just talking to each other and consider everybody else just, you know, not qualified to have any...

AD To enter into the dialogue.

FW That's right, exactly. So, I think that's it, with regard to your question about history... Besides wanting to do the works that I did with museums and have continued to do—just sort of slap people around and wake them up—it made me look at history—to see why is it this way and why there are things they're not talking about. So mostly, at that time, I was interested in colonialism in Africa and the history of Africa because I had been to West Africa studying art and dance in 1975. So I really... I just wanted to unpack it a little bit. In Africa I was studying African crafts, African tribal art and dance in various communities with artists, and historic African art as well as contemporary African art in different universities. I remember that once I was in an art class with African students, and they were doing these impressionist paintings. And I'm saying to myself, "These are really bad paintings and these folks have no connection to the reality of the history of this." And then it just flipped for me: What was Picasso's knowledge of these African art histories... Of the history and cultural philosophy of the images that he was using—were they as far-fetched, or much more about Europe than they were about what he was getting from Africa? And from an African perspective, would Picasso's work seem bad or meaningless? And was it the same as these students painting European-style paintings? What were they getting? Were they getting a European knowledge, or were they just recreating themselves through these foreign images? And it's all embedded in who they were. You know, I never answered that question, but it was... eye-opening and mind-expanding. Going to Africa really was a major mental shift for me. I saw a world that was completely different, but extremely inspiring at a very impressionable age. It bore no resemblance to what America told us Africa was. So it was making me question a lot. How could this happen? [chuckle] You know, the mythic story of Cubism and Africa, how could this happen... anthropology and art museums continuing subtle and often unsubtle demeaning, misleading interpretations and rationalizations for the public to absorb? How could, you know, what happened, happen? How come museums did not deal with Europe's devastating effect on the culture and life in Africa? Could it be that they feared being implicated? Or did they just not care?

And so all this is where my practice came from. And—you got me talking—I remember I worked in East Harlem. If you went over just a few blocks the Guggenheim Museum loomed. And my students and the teenagers never went over there... It was just, it was like...

AD Another world.

FW Yes. "That's another world, I'm a nobody there, I'm a somebody here, so I'm not going out." And this is Manhattan, you could walk! They never went downtown. And then of course vice versa.

AD Right—the people visiting the Guggenheim probably weren't going over to East Harlem!

FW No, no, and it was like a few blocks away. So these were right next to each other, but really separate. And so all this, this really got me going, and this is why I do what I do. And it still is important to me, but in different ways. Things become more personal, but it's still one of those things.

AD So your work and your interests came from your early visits to museums, obviously the trip to Africa, and just noticing how different the visitor, an African American visitor, felt in these spaces.

FW Yes. And you know, as a visitor to Africa I... It made me very hyper-aware that I am not African... And so it was all very interesting.

AD It's so terrific, and moving, to hear about this from you, your beginnings and early influences. I'm transitioning here, but I want now to ask about the title of the exhibition *Black to the Powers of Ten*, which refers to two short documentary films by Charles and Ray Eames. How did you decide upon that title in relation to the works on view?

FW I love titles and I hate titles because you have to really work at it, because you make the work and then you need to think about what to call it... But I was so happy with this title. I want to use it again, because it really does sum it up. Looking at this exhibition that's the combination of so many different things, works from different periods, I did notice that there is a macro view, it goes from the micro to the macro. I think it's all really in the prints that I did, very specifically, I could just name the print series that. But I think it's also a metaphor for everything else that I do, but the prints, they're basically just acid drips onto a plate, with black ink. It just looks like spots, or, for me, microbes or the galaxy.

AD Almost like a nebula.

FW Yeah, exactly. So it's looking at the micro and the macro, looking at the universe, and the tiniest things that cannot be seen by the naked eye, and all related to the color black. And so that, to me, was a metaphor for the prints, but also for the whole exhibition, because I don't limit it in thinking about these things. The universe is, for our naked eyes, black, and it's not that way in reality, it's really bright because of all the stars—if you could see. It's just because our eyes cannot see it all at once. So that is always in my thinking as well. In fact, my piece—which I always find difficult to pronounce—the *Othello* mirror sculpture, *Exeunt Omnes*, it's about the end of the play (page 82, right).

AD Right, "everyone walks off stage".

FW "Everyone walks off stage", and to me, the stage is dark, it's black, and it's quiet, and the stage is large. And so to me this was the sadness on top of the sadness, because it's over...

AD Yes, it's a terrible tragedy... and then it's over.

FW It's over, and it's dark, it's quiet, and you had to go back to your life, and so for me that piece embodies all that. And I only brought that up because we're talking about the universe being black, so it's not just about black people, or black objects, or materials. For me, the reason why black initially was so... I'm getting off on a tangent...

AD It's okay.

FW It's that initially it was a negative concept, because people are afraid of the dark, and with reason. There's a real strong reason to be afraid of the dark, because you don't know what's coming. But in a technological world that's sort of changed. We're not as afraid of the dark because we can control it. We think we're controlling it. And so it has been able to mean a lot of different things, including positive. It's not necessarily negative, but positive, and we can flirt with danger in nightlife. And it has multiple meanings now, more than it did before. However, technology is not the only way humans have overcome the fear of the dark. The Mbuti Pygmies have an old saying: "There is darkness all around us; but if darkness *is,* and the darkness is of the forest, then the darkness must be good."

AD That's really interesting—and of course shows there's more than one way to look at it.

FW From that philosophical statement, perhaps we could imagine that Ota Benga, the Mbuti Pygmy whose life cast portrait I made into a sculpture (page 79), bravely came, or was brought, to the U.S. understanding that there must be some goodness in things that are frighteningly unknown. But while his life was tenuous enough in the Belgian Congo, his life in the U.S. proved to be equally so—and worse. The indignities after indignities, which included the obligatory life cast done by the American Museum of Natural History while he was exhibited at the 1904 St. Louis World's Fair, and his subsequent display in the monkey cage at the Bronx Zoo, coupled with profound loneliness, were too much for him, and he committed suicide in Virginia at age 32.

AD It's a terrible, tragic story.

FW I could not leave him there, in the Hood Museum storage building where I found him when I was working on a project at Dartmouth. I recast the chipped plaster life cast in bronze, and it retains the chips, and his searching, straightforward look. I recast the bust to honor him and keep his memory alive, while at the same time not obscuring the tragedy wrought by time and the various museums he came in contact with.

Hmm . . . I just thought of something. As far as I know, there is no Pygmy flag. The pygmy communities are spread around various countries in Africa and they traditionally live nomadically in forests or now, sadly, on the fringes of society. If there were, it probably would include the color black: black representing the people and black representing the forest. Perhaps I should create one.

AD We are so happy to have your Ota Benga bust in the exhibition—it's an incredibly powerful work. Speaking of blackness and its importance in your work, the Allen Memorial Art Museum is about to purchase the first work by you to enter its permanent collection, *LIBERATION* (page 76, left). What is the importance and meaning to you of that work, in and of itself certainly, but then also in relation to your other flag paintings and your drips?

FW Well, I like that it combines the two. *LIBERATION* is actually the Black Liberation flag . . .

AD Yes, the Pan-African flag.

FW Yes, the African American, Black Liberation flag and also the Pan-African flag. Without the color, you just have the black stripe, but then there's the glass; I did want to combine these things, but the glass kind of animates it. I think it's funny, but also serious, and sad. It's just about liberation in general. But the pun is that the black is being liberated, literally.

AD Literally "liberated" out of the canvas, through the drips.

FW That's right. And if you look at it, if tears are part of it, the unfinished business of liberation is embedded in that flag. I could talk more about it, but those are the essential things that I was thinking about.

AD Thank you. We are so happy to have this work join the museum's permanent collection.

We're conducting this interview just two days after your sixty-second birthday, and such days naturally make one think both of the past and the future. What do you see as next for you in your practice? And what are you most proud of, in what has come before?

FW Well, let's just say this, artists don't really think about what they're going to do next, you live in the moment. At least, I think, if you live in the moment, maybe not in every aspect of your life, but certainly in art making, if you live in the moment, the future takes care of itself. So that's how I am with my work. I mean, obviously there are things I'm interested in, ideas and materials I'd like to work with, but they're just floating out there. They're floating out there, and eventually they'll stick when they're supposed to stick. But it's just not what an artist would do, to say, "Well in five years I'll be making this kind of painting or sculpture." There are things I've been working on and thinking about for a long time that will or won't come to fruition. But it's not like I can imagine something else...

AD Right, right now, what it's going to be.

FW No.

AD Well, we're coming to end of this interview, and I just wonder if there is anything more that you'd want to say about these exhibitions that we haven't already said? And if there is, that's great, and if not, that's okay too.

FW Right. Well, just to get sappy... My works are only as good as the people I talk to, the people I work with, the availability, and people's goodwill toward making it happen. And it's been a really special experience here. So I really feel strongly that working with all of you, the staff and the faculty, and everyone... It just makes for a very good project.

AD I agree.

FW It makes for a very... It's the best kind of way to make art.

AD It's been absolutely terrific. And I can certainly speak for all of the staff of the museum, from myself and Denise Birkhofer, to everyone on staff—everyone in the museum has worked on these exhibitions in some way—as well as faculty and students. It's been a tremendous experience to work with you, Fred. And we could not thank you more.

FW Oh thank you. [chuckle]

AD Thank you.

1. Angèle Waton, *Negro Family*, ca. 1930, Anonymous Gift, 1938.24, and American, *Mechanical Box with Automaton*, 1880s, Gift of Gladys Sellew, 1958.160. Both works are in the exhibition.

2. François-Auguste-René Rodin, *The Prodigal Son*, c. 1905, R. T. Miller Jr. Fund, 1955.32, and Japanese, *Coiling Dragon*, late 19th century, Gift of Charles F. Olney, 1904.723A–C. Neither work is in the exhibition.

3. Afghan, *Seated Buddha*, 5th century, R. T. Miller Jr. Fund, 1946.25. The wooden base for this work is in the exhibition, but the Buddha figure is not.

4. Thomas Satterwhite Noble, *The Present*, 1865, R. T. Miller Jr. Fund and James K. (OC 1946) and Anne Fassett (OC 1947) Sunshine American Art Fund. 2014.30. This work is in the exhibition.

5. Sir Thomas Lawrence, *Portrait of Eleanor, Lady Wigram*, 1815–16, R. T. Miller Jr. Fund and Mrs. F. F. Prentiss Fund in memory of Chloe Hamilton Young, 1986.17, and *Portrait of Sir Robert Wigram, 1st Baron, MP*, 1815–16, R. T. Miller Jr. Fund, 2010.14.

6. Douglas Baxter, an Oberlin alumnus of 1972 and longstanding member of the Allen Memorial Art Musuem's Visiting Committee, is the President of Pace Gallery.

7. The casts were not at that time on view at the museum. Some were on view in the Clarence Ward Art Library, and the stairwell leading to it.

8. Lewis's drawing is similar to a sculpture of a seated Urania in the Museo Nazionale Romano, Palazzo Altemps, Rome.

9. Above the east side of the King Sculpture Court is a small balcony (pages 34–35, top).

10. Lewis's *The Death of Cleopatra* (1876, Smithsonian American Art Museum 1994.17) was exhibited at the Allen Memorial Art Museum from 2001 to 2004; see Birkhofer's essay in this catalogue for a brief history of its vicissitudes.

11. On February 27, 2016, Wilson and Derstine attended the symposium "Complicated Relationships: Mary Church Terrell's Legacy for 21st Century Activists," organized by Oberlin College professors Pam Brooks and Carol Lasser and co-sponsored by the Oberlin College Archives, the college's Gender, Sexuality and Feminist Studies program, the Africana Studies and History Departments, the Oberlin Alumni Association of African Ancestry (OA4), and the Office of Alumni Relations. Terrell, an Oberlin College alumna of the class of 1884, was a feminist and civil rights activist and a founding member of the National Association of Colored Women and the National Association for the Advancement of Colored People.

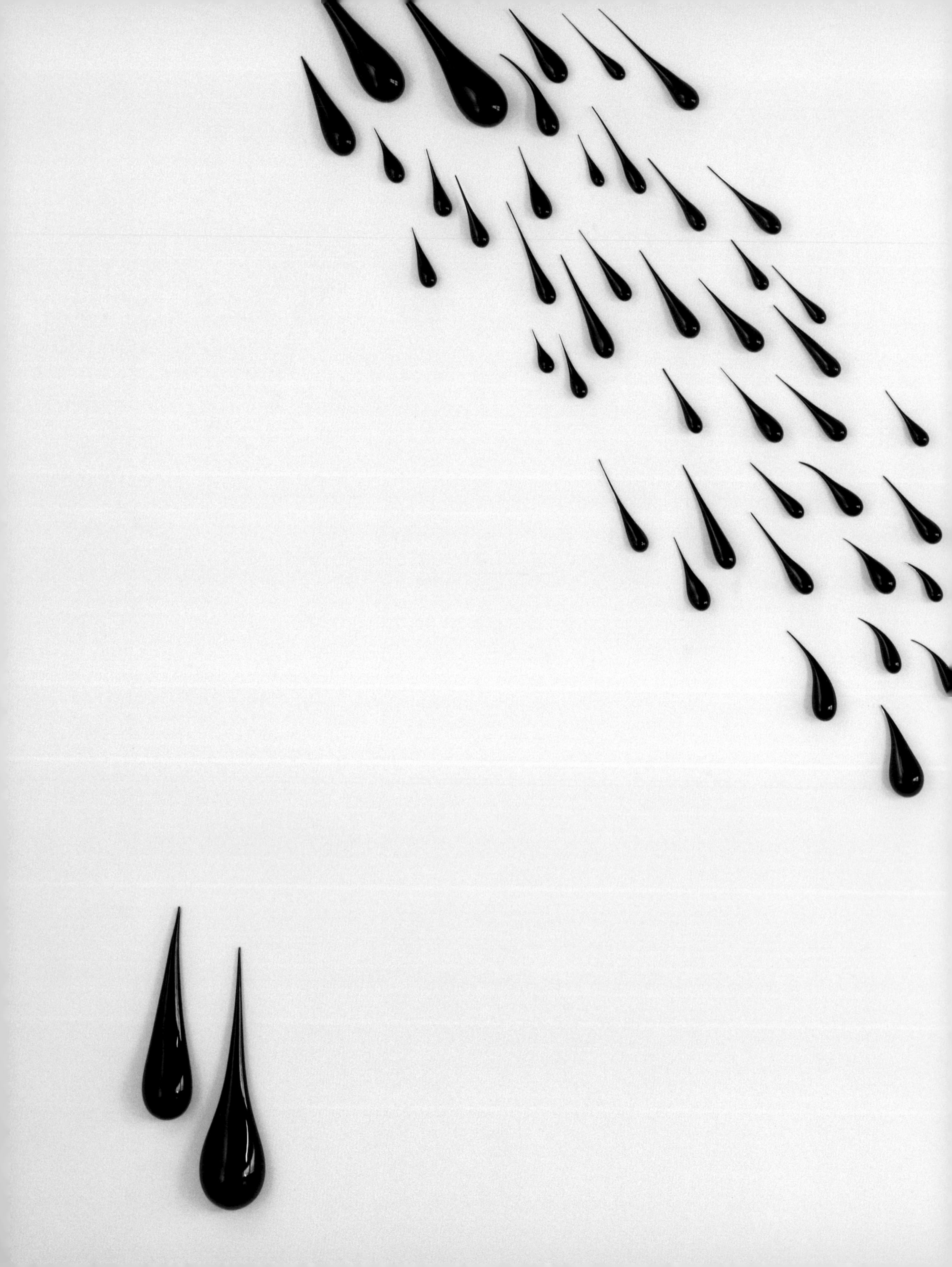

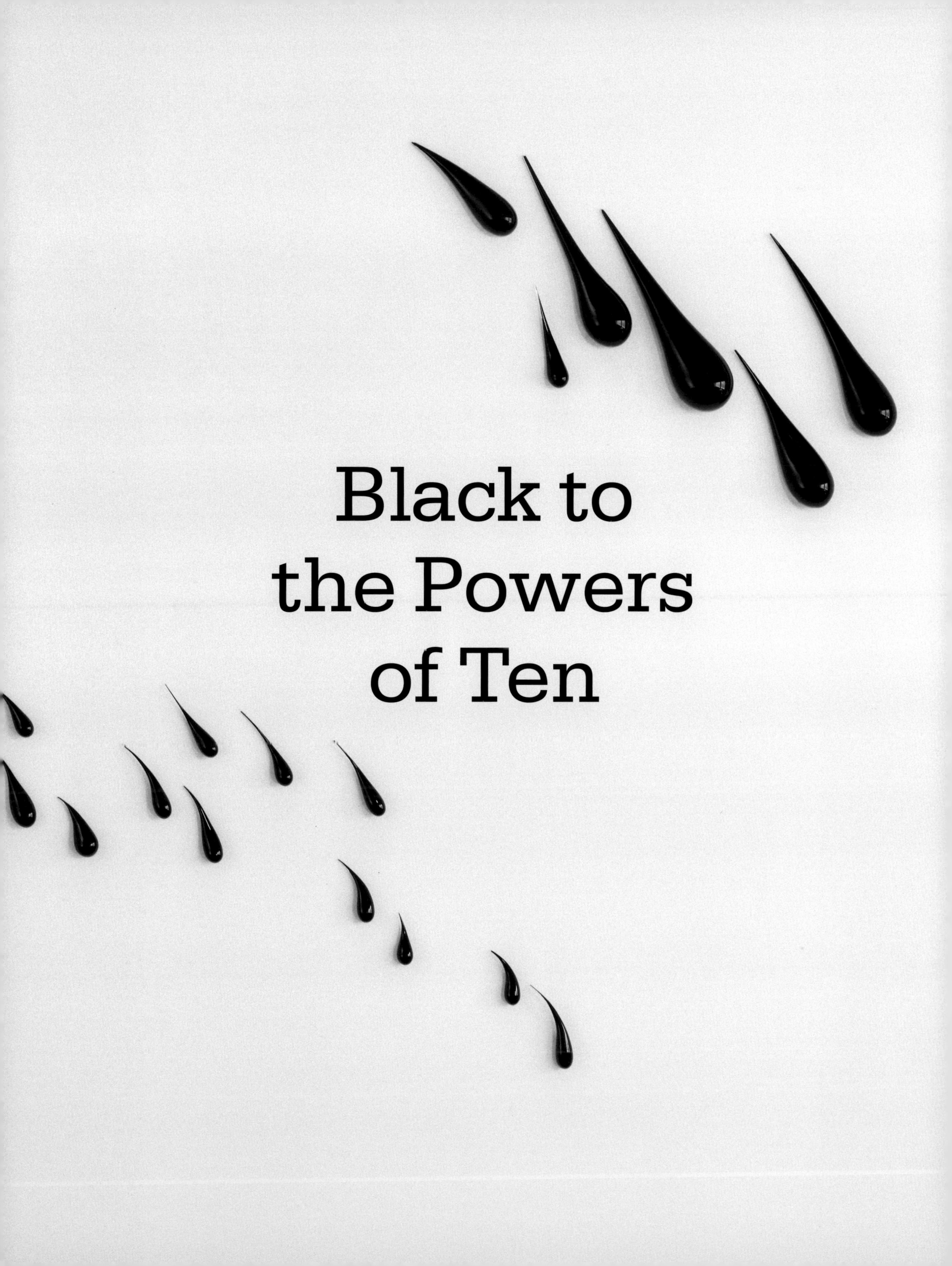

Black to the Powers of Ten

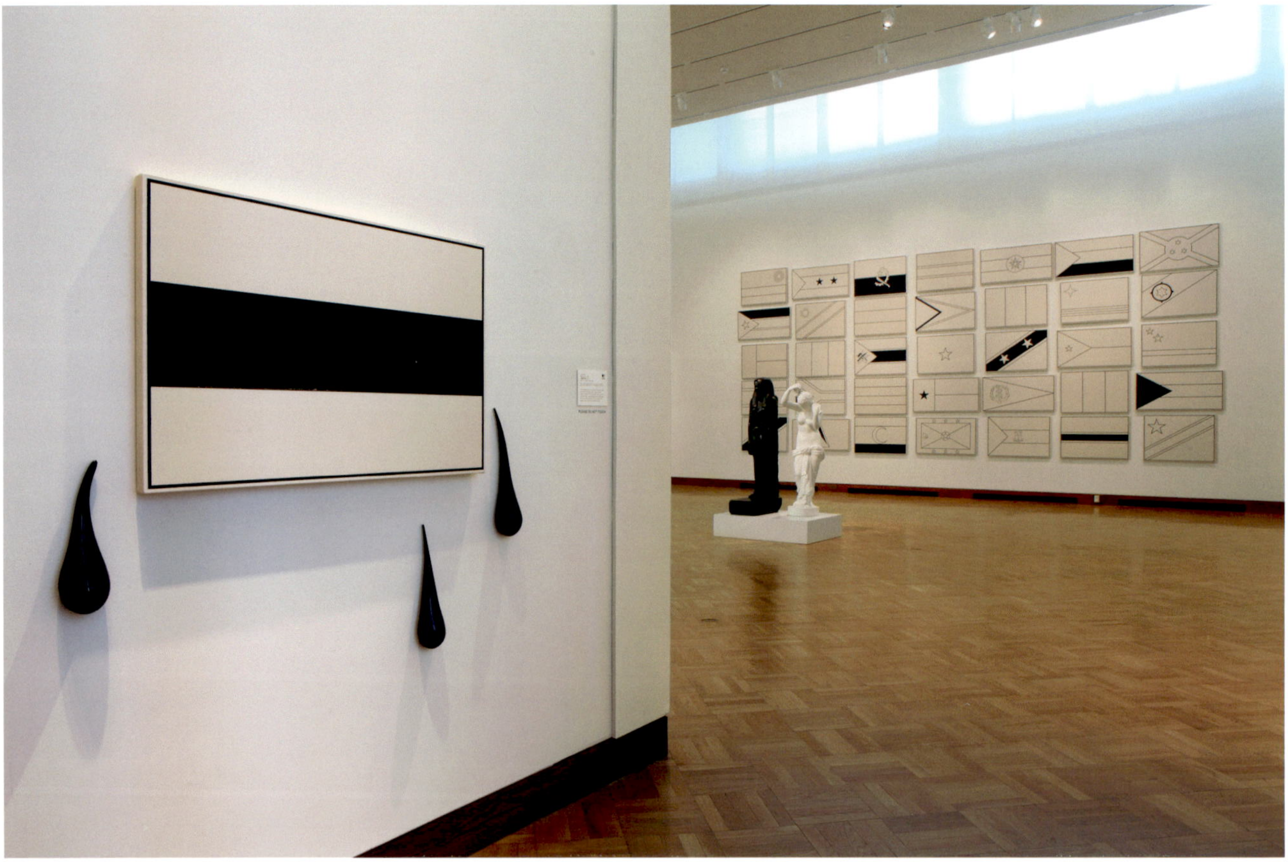

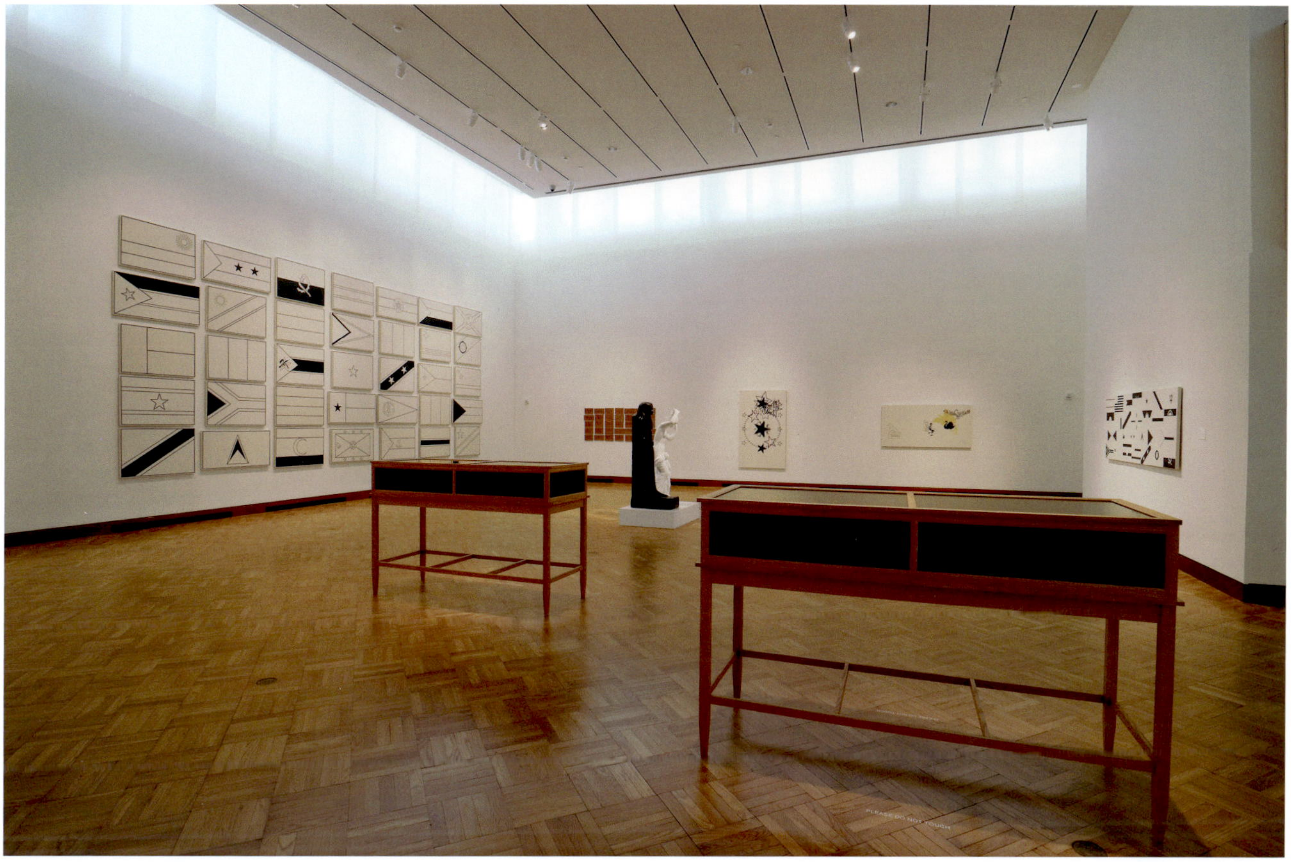

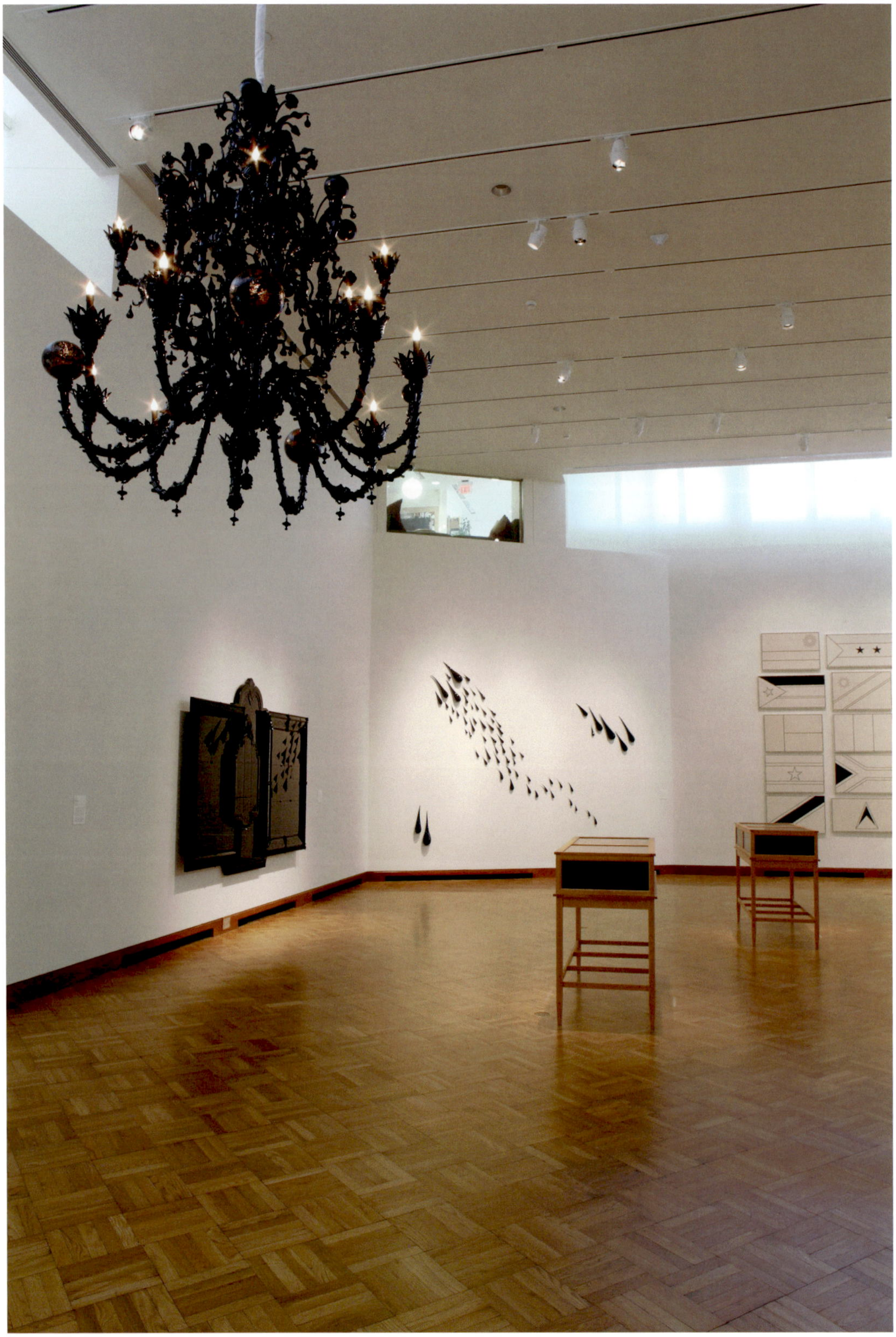

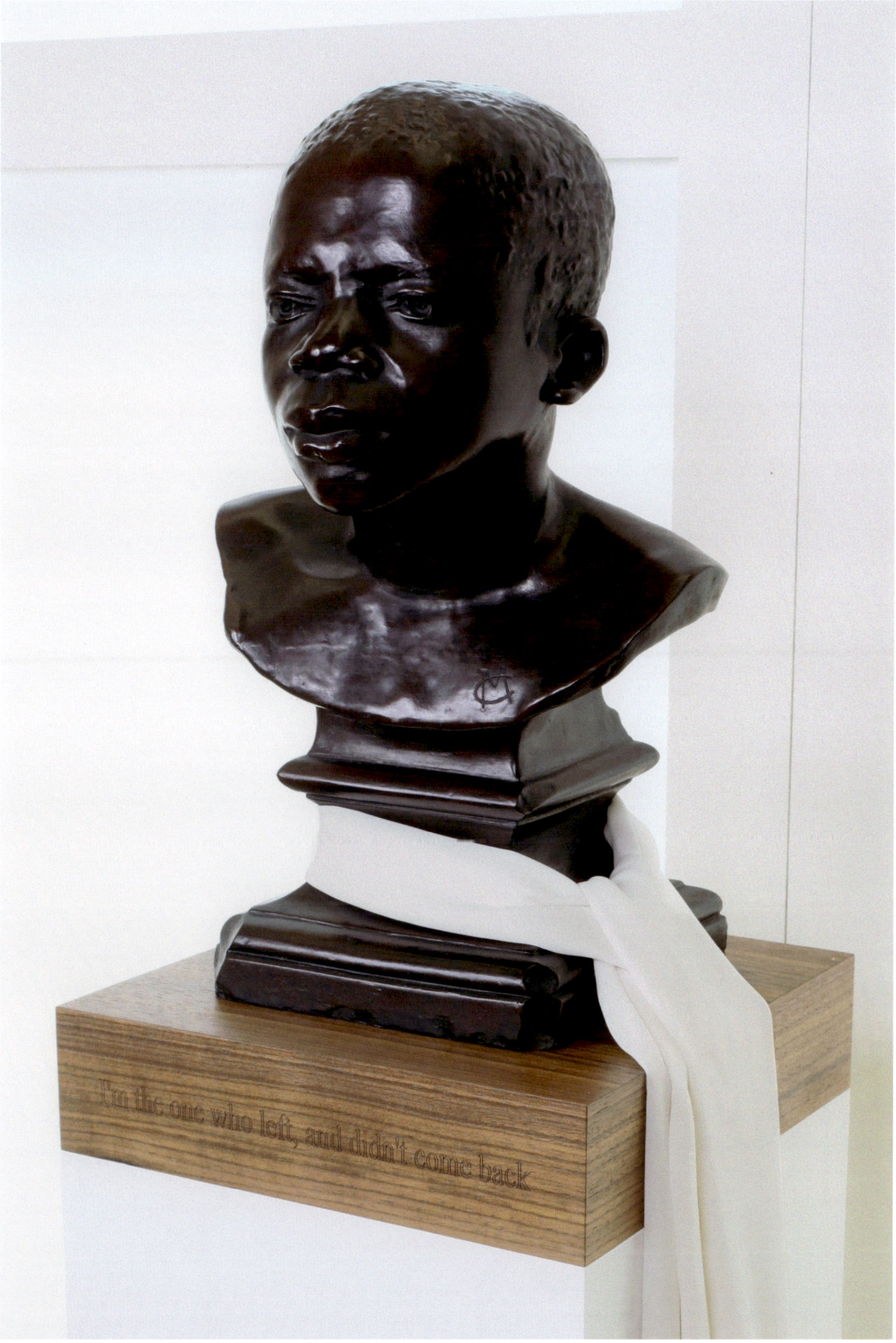
I'm the one who left, and didn't come back

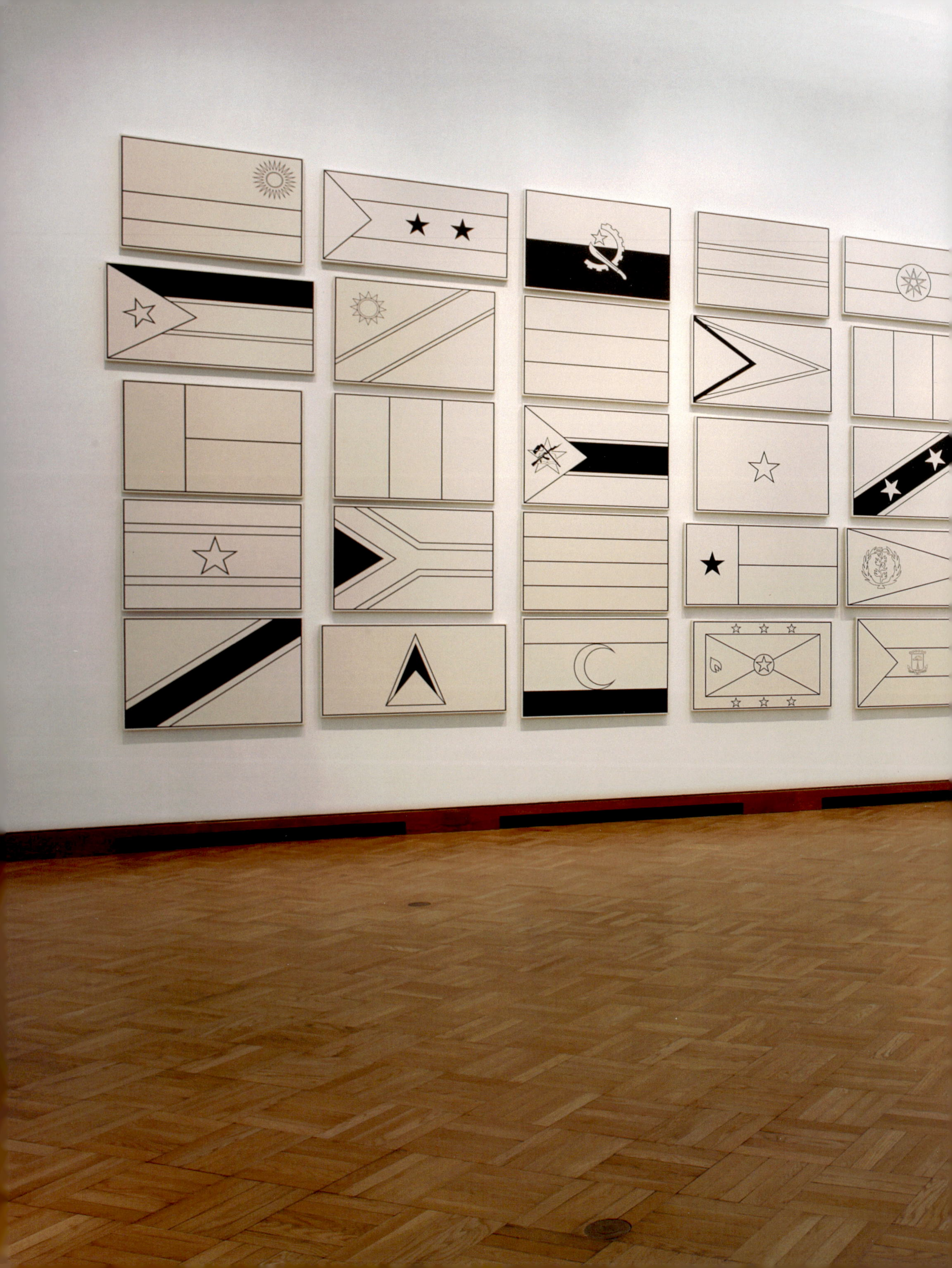

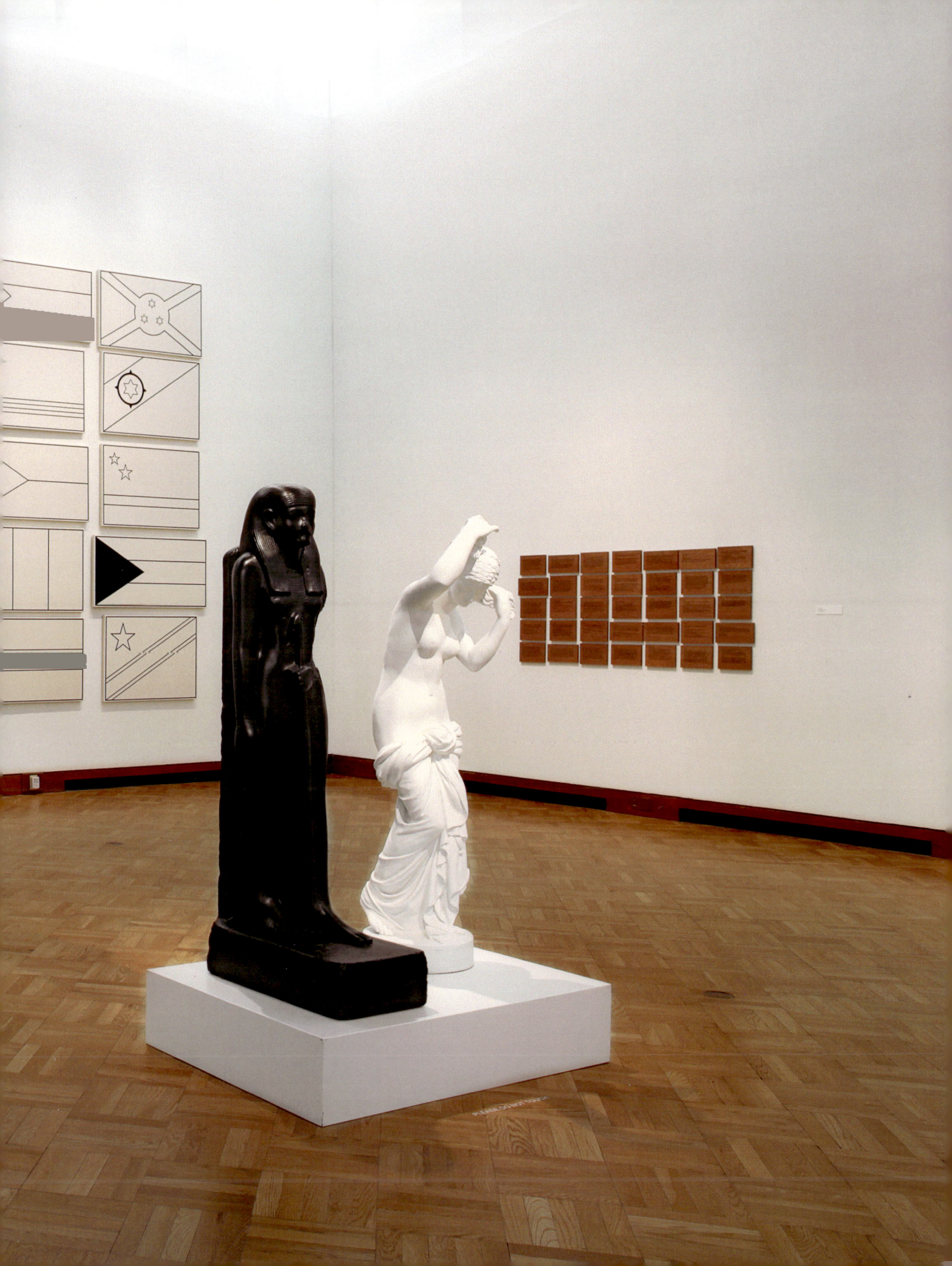

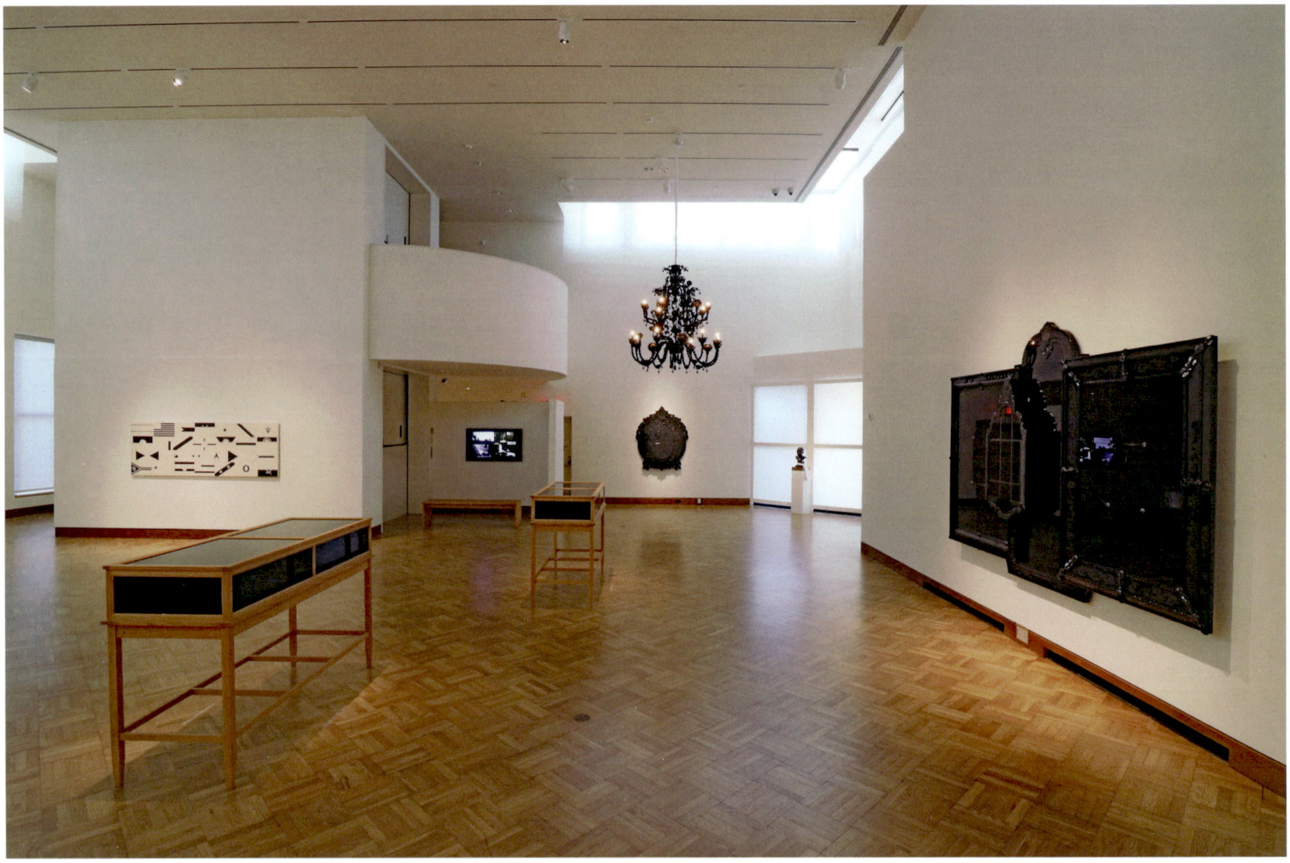

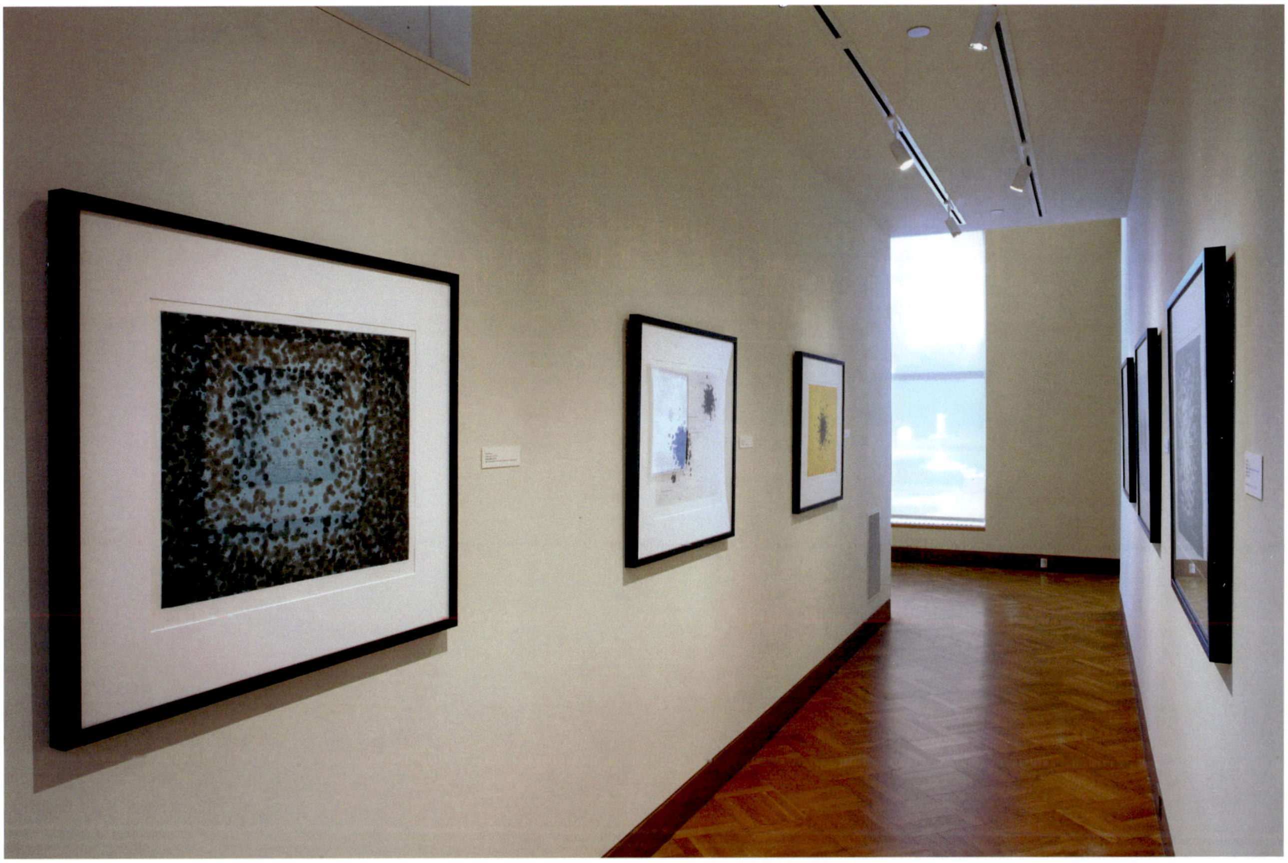

Checklists of the Exhibitions

(in chronological order)

Wildfire Test Pit

Austrian, *St. Michael Weighing Souls*, ca. 1470, tempera on panel. R.T. Miller Jr. Fund, 1943.113

Unknown, *Adoration of the Magi*, date unknown, possibly 18th century, oil on canvas. Anonymous Gift in Honor of Margaret Schauffler, UN1982.5

Washington Allston (American, 1779–1843), *Tavern Scene*, 1811–18, pencil and oil sketch on canvas. Gift of Henry L. de Rham as trustee of the Dana Collection of Allston Pictures, 1956.17

Unknown carver, *Gravestone of Lee Howard Dobbins*, 1853, sandstone. Courtesy of Oberlin College Library Special Collections

Edmonia Lewis (American, 1844–1907), *Untitled drawing after Urania, the Greek Muse of Astronomy*, 1862, reproduction of original pencil drawing on buff paper. Courtesy of the Oberlin College Archives

Thomas Satterwhite Noble (American, 1835–1907), *The Present*, 1865, oil on canvas. R.T. Miller Jr. Fund and James K. (OC 1946) and Anne Fassett (OC 1947) Sunshine American Art Fund, 2014.30

Joseph-Charles de Blézer (French, active 1860–85), *Bust of John Brown*, 1870, bronze. Courtesy of the Oberlin College Archives

Edmonia Lewis (American, 1844–1907), *Bust of James Peck Thomas*, 1874, marble. R.T. Miller Jr. Fund, 2002.3

American, *Mechanical Box with Automaton*, 1880s, cardboard box with print, sand, figurines. Gift of Gladys Sellew, 1958.160

Nicholas Alden Brooks (American, active 1880–1904), *Handbill of the Play at the Night of Lincoln's Assassination*, 1893, oil on oak panel. Gift of Charles F. Olney, 1904.593

Baga artist, *Headdress (Nimba)*, late 19th–early 20th century, wood. Gift of Gustave Schindler, 1958.175

American Indian, Sioux, *Pair of Moccasins*, late 19th–early 20th century, leather and multicolored beads. Gift of the Oberlin College Department of Zoology, 1957.134 A-B

American Indian, Cheyenne, *Pair of Moccasins*, late 19th–early 20th century, leather with yellow, blue, and white beads. Gift of the Oberlin College Department of Zoology, 1957.133 A-B

Giorgio de Chirico (Italian, born in Greece, 1888–1978), *La Solitudine*, ca. 1915, oil on canvas. Gift of Priscilla and Richard Hunt in memory of President and Mrs. William E. Stevenson, 1988.23

School of Phidias (Greek, active 465–425 BC), *Block 1 from the West Frieze of the Parthenon*, 1917 cast of 5th century BC original in the British Museum, plaster cast. Allen Memorial Art Museum, 1917.22.1

Phidias (Greek, active 465–425 BC), *Two Fates (Artemis and Aphrodite), from the East Pediment of the Parthenon, Athens, Greece*, 1917 cast of 5th century BC original in the British Museum, London, plaster cast. Allen Memorial Art Museum, 1917.23

Praxiteles (Greek, active 4th century BC), *Artemis of Gabii*, 1917 cast of 4th century BC original in the Louvre, Paris, plaster cast. Allen Memorial Art Museum, 1917.25

Praxiteles (Greek, active 4th century BC), *Hermes and the Infant Dionysius*, 1917 cast of 4th century BC original in the Archaeological Museum, Olympia, Rome, plaster cast. Allen Memorial Art Museum, 1917.28

Alexandros of Antioch (Greek, active 2nd century BC), *Venus of Milos*, 1917 cast of 2nd century BC original in the Louvre, Paris, plaster cast. Allen Memorial Art Museum, 1917.30

Greek, *Sleeping Erinnys*, 1917 cast of a 2nd century AD Roman copy in the Museo Nationale Romano, Palazzo Altemps, of a 4th century BC original, plaster cast. Allen Memorial Art Museum, 1917.26

Jacopo della Quercia (Italian, ca. 1374–1438), *Ilaria del Carretto*, 1917 cast of ca. 1406 original, plaster cast. Allen Memorial Art Museum, 1917.45

Donatello (Italian, 1386–1466), *David*, 1917 cast of ca. 1440 original in the National Museum of the Bargello, Florence, plaster cast. Allen Memorial Art Museum, 1917.41

Andrea del Verrocchio (Italian, 1435–1488), *David*, 1917 cast of 1473–75 original in the National Museum of the Bargello, Florence, plaster cast. Allen Memorial Art Museum, 1917.42

Andrea della Robbia (Italian, 1435–1525), *The Annunciation*, 1917 cast of ca. 1490 original, plaster cast. Allen Memorial Art Museum, 1917.36 A-C

H. D. Thrasher (American, 1883–1918), *Prentiss Family Memorial in the form of a Greek Stele Representing Rectitude and Love*, ca. 1917, plaster cast. Gift of Kenyon Cox, 1917.11

Richmond Barthé (American, 1901–1989), *Head of a Negro*, 1924–28, bronze-colored terracotta. Anonymous Gift, 1939.6

Angèle Watson (Belgian, 1886/87–1980), *Negro Family*, ca. 1930, oil on canvas. Anonymous Gift, 1938.24

Richmond Barthé (American, 1901–1989), *African Head*, ca. 1935, terracotta. Gift of Mrs. Malcolm L. McBride, 1946.50

George Segal (American, 1924–2000), *Black Girl, Black Doorframe*, 1978, painted wood and plaster. Gift of Jane S. Murray, 1986.46

Baule artist, Ivory Coast, *Face Mask (Kpan)*, 20th century, wood. Gift in honor of Alexandra Gould (OC 2011), 2011.26.13

Baule artist, Ivory Coast, *Female Figure*, 20th century, wood and gold leaf. Gift in honor of Alexandra Gould (OC 2011), 2011.26.10

Luba artist, Democratic Republic of the Congo, *Zoomorphic Mask*, early to mid-20th century, wood. Gift in honor of Alexandra Gould (OC 2011), 2011.26.34

Mende artist, *Sande Society Mask (Sowei)*, 20th century, wood and raffia. Gift in honor of Alexandra Gould (OC 2011), 2011.26.35

Mumuye artist, Nigeria, *Iagalagana (Female Figure)*, 20th century, wood and kaolin. Gift in honor of Alexandra Gould (OC 2011), 2011.26.18

Yorùbá artist, *Gelede Female Torso Mask*, 20th century, wood with pigment. Gift in honor of Dr. George Eaton Simpson, 2000.1

Rev. Albert Wagner (American, 1924–2006), *Ethiopia*, late 20th century, acrylic, ink, oil stick, and graphite on canvas. Ruth C. Roush Contemporary Art Fund, 2012.20

Base for Afghan *Seated Buddha* (5th century, R.T. Miller Jr. Fund, 1946.25), wood, 20th century

Four African figures, possibly 20th century, wood, standing in rock salt. Collection of Fred Wilson

Numerous plaster cast fragments, 20th and 21st century, Courtesy of Nicholas Fairplay, Fairplay Stonecarvers L.L.C., Oberlin, Ohio

Fred Wilson (American, b. 1954), *Grinding Souls*, 2016, sandstone grindstone and brass figures. Gift of the artist, 2016.46.1 A-K

Fred Wilson (American, b. 1954), *The Apoxyomenos*, 2016, metal trash can and rock salt. Gift of the artist, 2016.46.2 A-B

Two telescopes. Allen Memorial Art Museum purchases

Fred Wilson: Black to the Powers of Ten

All works by Fred Wilson (American, b. 1954), and courtesy of the artist and Pace Gallery, except as noted below.

September Dream, 2003, four-channel digital video, 6 minutes and 31 seconds

Arise!, 2004, spit bite aquatint with direct gravure

Bang, 2004, spit bite aquatint with color aquatint

Convocation, 2004, spit bite aquatint with color aquatint and direct gravure

Dawn, 2004, spit bite aquatint with gampi paper chine collé

Exchange, 2004, spit bite aquatint with color aquatint and direct gravure

We Are All in the Gutter, But Some of Us Are Looking at the Stars, 2004, spit bite aquatint

Black Memory, 2005, glass bottle, ink wells, and oil cans installed in wood and glass vitrine

Black Present, 2006, ink wells, oil cans, and resin skeleton installed in wood and glass vitrine

The Mete of the Muse, 2006, bronze with black patina and bronze with white paint

Ota Benga, 2008, bronze with silk scarf and wood base. Collection of Douglas Baxter (OC 1972)

Bat, 2009, Murano glass and wood. Private collection

Black Flags, 2009, acrylic on canvas

Black Plaques, 2009, wooden plaques

The People, 2010, acrylic on canvas

LIBERATION, 2012, acrylic on canvas, blown glass. Ruth C. Roush Contemporary Art Fund, and gift of the artist and Pace Gallery, Douglas Baxter (OC 1972), President, 2016.30A-D

I Saw Othello's Visage in His Mind, 2013, Murano glass and wood

No Way But This, 2013, Murano glass and light bulbs

Black All Stars, 2014, acrylic on canvas

Black Birds, 2014, acrylic and graphite on canvas

Act V. Scene II – Exeunt Omnes, 2014, Murano glass and wood

Whether or Not, 2014, blown glass

Wildfire Test Pit Display Text

Integral to Fred Wilson's *Wildfire Test Pit* is the use of large display text about the life and work of sculptor Edmonia Lewis. In long lines of running text on the uppermost part of the gallery walls, he commingles Lewis's time at Oberlin College with the later fate of some of her works during the 20th century. Elsewhere, Wilson gives us a chronology of places that Lewis lived and worked, a list of the sitters for her marble portrait busts, and a list of women in her expatriate community in Rome. He also pulls verses from a transcendentalist poem painted on the museum's clerestory and uses a slogan that appears on the façade of the 1917 building. The complete display text from the exhibition is reproduced here.

THE CAUSE OF ART IS THE CAUSE OF THE PEOPLE

This letter is to formally notify you of the damage in transit...

One evening she stepped out into the dark, she was seized, dragged to a nearby empty field, and brutally thrashed...

...Lying in the cold, her clothing torn and her body terribly beaten.

...As it lay there, deteriorating, it was spotted by Harold Adams, a local fire inspector.

There...resting among paint cans and discarded Christmas decorations, covered with paint, and scarred by weather and vandalism

...He only said, "The Queen is not ready to receive visitors."

...the Egyptian queen turned up in a shopping mall warehouse.

...is in extremely poor condition.

There is a large hole in the chest area and both arms...broken off and are in numerous...

...fate, it seems, is bound inextricably by the forces of politics and history.

Yet, even at this desolate moment, as her right hand...

The decline of native peoples was seen as romantic but inevitable...

1859–62—Oberlin College, Rev. John Keep's house, 154 North Main Street; 1864—Boston, studio building, 89 Tremont Street; 1867—Rome, home studio, 57 via della Frezza, 4 via XX Settembre, 7 via Gregoriana; 1873—Boston, residence, 40 Poplar Street; 1901—London, England, Tottenham Court Road; 1905–7—London, England, 4a Earl's Court Road, Victorian Brick House, 154 Blythe Road; 1907—London, England, Kensal Green Cemetery

Dr. Hebbard
Henry Longfellow
Charles Sumner
John Brown
William Lloyd Garrison
Robert Gould Shaw
Voltaire
President Lincoln
Horace Greeley
Gerrit Smith
Dr. Bowditch
Dioclesian Lewis
General Ulysses Grant
Bishop Foley
John Brown
Bishop A. D. Payne
Harriet Hosmer
Charlotte Cushman
Maria Weston Chapman
Anne Quincy Waterson
James Peck Thomas
Frederick Douglass
James McCune Smith

Thought is deeper than all speech,
Feeling deeper than all thought;
Souls to souls can never teach
What unto themselves was taught.
Heart to heart was never known;
Mind with mind did never meet;
We are columns left alone
Of a temple once complete.

Edmonia Lewis (1843–1907), Sarah Clampitt Ames (1817–1901), Louisa Lander (1826–1923), Emma Stebbins (1815–1882), Margaret Foley (1827–1877), Florence Freeman (1836–1876), Anne Whitney (1821–1915), Blanche Nevin (1838–1925), Vinnie Ream Hoxie (1847–1914), and Harriet Hosmer (1830–1908).

In addition to standard labels identifying objects in the *Wildfire Test Pit* exhibition, Wilson produced more than thirty labels taken from the footnote entries of a variety of scholars writing on Edmonia Lewis and related subjects. These are installed throughout the exhibition, providing an extra layer of context and meaning.

[207] Frederick Douglass, editorial, "Miss Edmonia Lewis."

[499] Oberlin College purchased the Thomas bust in 2002. See also Flotte, "Edmonia Lewis," which described restoring it. See also John Hope Franklin and Loren Schweninger, *In Search of the Promised Land. Slave Family in the Old South* (New York: Oxford University Press, 2006), 19, 240–241. In Dred Scott v. Sandford, 1857, the U.S. Supreme Court ruled that all people of African descent could never be U.S. citizens. The Fourteenth Amendment overruled it in 1868.

13. J. S. Kasson, *Marble Queens and Captives: Women in Nineteenth-Century American Sculpture* (New Haven, 1990), 142–147. Albert Boime, (*The Art of Exclusion: Representing Blacks, in the Nineteenth Century* [Washington, D.C., 1990], 236, n. 30) cites an 1873 description of Lewis that stated, "Her appearance is masculine and her voice hard and gruff."

12. H.W. 1866 (note 5). An 1871 interviewer also noted that "her manners are childlike, simple, and most winning and pleasing," see Bullard 1871 (note 6).

[39] Official documents being lost, the contemporary record of the incident, which took place Jan. 27, 1862, and its aftermath came mainly via news coverage and a diary: *Cleveland (OH) Plain Dealer*, "Mysterious Affair at Oberlin," Feb. 11, 1862, "Oberlin Poisoning Case," Feb. 25, 1862, and "Oberlin Poisoning Case Again," Mar. 3, 1862; LCN, "Trial in Prospect," Feb. 19, 1862, "Poisoning Affair," Mar. 5; *Cleveland (OH) Morning Leader*, "Oberlin Poisoning Case," Mar. 3, 1862; Fannie

Maria White [Mrs. James Bailey]. Diary, Jan. 31, 1862, Oberlin College Archives. See also Langston, Virginia Plantation, 171–180; Blodgett, "John Mercer Langston" and "Spiced Wine."

17. Hazel V. Carby, *Reconstructing Womanhood: The Emergence of the Afro-American Woman Novelist* (New York, 1987), 25: Karen Sanhez-Eppler, "Bodily Bonds: The Intersecting Rhetorics of Feminism and Abolitionism," *Representations* 24 (September 1988): 39, Carolyn L. Karcher, "Rape, Murder and Revenge in 'Slavery's Pleasant Homes': Lydia Maria Child's Antislavery Fiction and the Limits of Genre," in *The Culture of Sentiment: Race, Gender, and Sentimentality in Nineteenth-Century America,* ed. Shirley Samuels (New York, 1992) 58–72. See also Judith Wilson, "Optical Illusions: Images of Miscegenation in Nineteenth- and Twentieth-Century Art," *American Art* 5 (Summer 1991): 89–107; and Patricia Morton, *Disfigured Images: The Historical Assault on Afro-American Women* (New York, 1991). For stereotyped images of Indian women as "squaws" and "princesses" see Rayna Green. " 'The Pocahontas Perplex': The Image of Indian Women in American Culture," in *Unequal Sisters: A Multicultural Reader in U.S. Women's History,* ed. Ellen C. DuBois and Vicki L. Ruiz (New York, 1990), 15-21: Julie Schimmel, "'Inventing the Indian'" in *The West as America: Reinterpreting Images of the Frontier 1820–1920,* ed. William H. Truettner (Washington, D.C., 1991), 149–89: and Asebrit Sundquist, *Pocahontas & Co.: The Fictional American Indian Woman in Nineteenth-Century Literature: A Study of Method* (Atlantic Highlands, N.J., 1987).

3. Harry Henderson and Romare Bearden (*A History of African-American Artists: From 1792 to the Present* [New York, 1993] 54, notes 4 and 5) cite circumstantial evidence that Edmonia was born in the Niagara region of upstate New York to a mother who was Mississauga Chippewa and had married "a colr [sic] man named Lewis." But the dating of their documentation seems to contradict Edmonia's birth date and her age when she entered Oberlin College. Also see M. Richardson, "Edmonia Lewis's *The Death of Cleopatra*: Myth and Identity," *The International Review of African American Art,* Summer 1995: 18–19.

Lysippus
(Greek, active 4th century BC)
The Apoxyomenos, 1917 cast of a 1st century AD Roman copy in the Vatican Museums of a 4th century BC original
Plaster

[44] Marcia Goldberg, "A Drawing by Edmonia Lewis," *American Art Journal* 9 (1977): 104; Marcia Goldberg and W.E. Bigglestone, "A Wedding Gift of 1862," *Oberlin Alumni Magazine,* Jan.–Feb. 1977, 20; J.V. Turano, "More Information on Edmonia Lewis' Drawing," *American Art Journal* 10 (1978): 112. See also Miller, *An Illustrated History,* 374–376.

21. "[It was] God's gift ... of unconquerable energy, as well as genius... [that enabled] her to rise above all prejudices of race or color, and command the respect and honor of all true lovers of art," quoted in Evan-Tibbs (note 9).

13. Harriet Beecher Stowe, for example, described Sojourner Truth interchangeably as African, Libyan, Ethiopian, and Egyptian; see Harriet Beecher Stowe, "Sojourner Truth, the Libyan Sibyl," *Atlantic Monthly* 11, no. 66 (April 1863): 473–81. Cleopatra's race was also the subject of an ongoing debate in the nineteenth century. See George M. Fredrickson, *The Black Image in the White Mind: The Debate on Afro-American Character and Destiny, 1877–1914* (New York, 1971), 74–75, 79; and Robert J. Young, *Colonial Desire: Hybridity in Theory, Culture and Race* (New York, 1995).

16. For example, once she had decided to sculpt a bust of Henry Longfellow, Lewis was so determined that she stalked her subject through the streets of Rome to catch his likeness until Longfellow's brother assisted her efforts by persuading the poet to sit for her, see Tufts 1987 (note 15), 107. For additional letters, see J. Holland, "Mary Edmonia Lewis and the Hierarchy of Gender and Race," in "Co-Workers in the Kingdom of Culture: Edward Mitchell Bannister and the Boston Community of African-American Artists, 1848–1901" (Ph.D. diss., Columbia University, 1995) 45–51, notes 129–148.

[445] Francis DeCurtis, Chicago History Museum, email May 30, 2008: The Bowen copy of Hagar, except for the hands, was destroyed by the Great Chicago Fire of 1871. The surviving fragment could not be located.

20. Film theory is particularly germane to understanding Lewis's frame of reference as a black female spectator. As important as what and how she chose to sculpt was what she chose not to sculpt—half-naked black and Indian women or the depressed and dying male Indians or savages that were so popular in the nineteenth century.

Quoting song lyrics by Nina Simone, this text was displayed near Joseph-Charles de Blézer's *Bust of John Brown,* an 1870 memorial to the abolitionist who—frustrated by the slow progress of the movement—advocated violent opposition to slavery:

They keep on saying 'Go slow!'
But that's just the trouble
TOO SLOW!
Washing the windows
TOO SLOW!
Picking the cotton
TOO SLOW!
You're just plain rotten
TOO SLOW!
Do things gradually
TOO SLOW!
Will bring more tragedy
TOO SLOW!
Why don't you see it?
Why don't you feel it?
I don't know
I don't know

Wilson displayed this text near the museum label for a terracotta bust by Richmond Barthé, once called *Shoeshine Boy* and now titled *Head of Negro,* and the *Gravestone of Lee Howard Dobbins,* symbolically linking the two works:

Head of a Boy
Head of an African American Boy
Portrait of an African American Boy
Portrait of Lee Howard Dobbins

28. Elizabeth Johns (*American Genre Painting: The Politics of Everyday Life* [New Haven, 1991], 63–64) has discussed how representations of Indians by white American painters expressed both European stereotypes of the noble primitive, as well as American fears of the barbarous savage; these images served to promulgate, for fascinated Eastern audiences, the idea of Native Americans as a vanishing race.

[623] *Newport (RI) Daily News*, Sept. 19, 1878, 4: "At the Centennial she was insulted and struck because she was a negress claiming to have done the works she did;" BDET, Art and Artists, Sept. 16, 1878, 6; *Atchison (KS) Globe*, Oct. 8, 1878, 1: DKJ, "Miss Edmonia Lewis," Oct. 21, 1878, 3.

[203] Blodgett, "John Mercer Langston." W.E. Bigglestone, Oberlin College archivist, Sept. 1981 visit, advised that fire destroyed records, 1846–1866.

16. Laura Mulvey, "Visual Pleasure and Narrative Cinema," in *Issues in Feminist Film Criticism*, ed. Patricia Erens (Bloomington, Ind., 1990), 29. Mulvey uses the term "bearers of meaning" to describe the female's function within narrative cinema: woman exists as a spectacle, an erotic object who often interprets narrative. Lewis, by contrast, inverted this formula by sculpting a nude male who, both masculinized and eroticized, functions as spectacle and who, by virtue of his hair, carries the mark of race. See also, Manthia Diawara, "Black Spectatorship: Problems of Identification and Resistance," in *Black American Cinema*, ed. Manthia Diawara (New York, 1993), 211–20; bell hooks, *Black Looks: Race and Representation* (Boston, 1992); Cheryl Butler, "The Color Purple Controversy: Black Woman Spectatorship," *Wide Angle* 13, no. {[FR]} ¾ [sic] (1991): 62–69; and Jane Gaines, "White Privilege and Looking Relations: Race and Gender in Feminist Film Theory," in Erens, *Issues*, 197–214.

Lewis was accused of poisoning her two white female roommates while a student at Oberlin College. Having been beaten in a field and left for dead, Lewis stood trial, was cleared of all charges, and left school the following year. For an overview of Edmonia Lewis's life, see Kirsten P. Buick, "Edmonia Lewis in Art History: The Paradox of the Exotic Subject," in *Three Generations of African American Women Sculptors: A Study in Paradox*, ed. Leslie King-Hammond and Tritobia Hayes Benjamin (Philadelphia: Afro-American Historical and Cultural Museum, 1996) pp. 12–17; and Kirsten P. Buick, "The Sentimental Education of Mary Edmonia Lewis: Identity, Culture, and Ideal Works" (Ph.D. dissertation, University of Michigan, 1999). See also Juanita Marie Holland, "Mary Edmonia Lewis's Minnehaha: Gender, Race and the 'Indian Maid,'" *Bulletin of the Detroit Institute of Arts* 62, nos. 1–2 (1995): 26–36.

20. She converted to Catholicism in 1868, and at some point was visited in her studio by Pope Pius IX, see L. R. Hartigan, *Sharing Traditions: Five Black Artists in Nineteenth-Century America* (Washington, D.C.: exh. cat. 1985), 94, and "An Unplaced Artist," *The Peoples' Advocate* (Washington D.C. December 4, 1880): 1. In the medium of sculpture, Erastus Dow Palmer's *The Indian Girl, or Dawn of Christianity* as well as Joseph Mozier's *Pocahontas* illustrated the transformative and overwhelming effects of Christianity upon the noble savage. Lewis's ambitions as a neoclassical sculptor and her devout embrace of Christianity affirmed, like those images, beliefs about the proper course for American Indians, and in particular the ability of the Native American woman to be saved and civilized through Christianity. See W. H. Gerdts, "The Marble Savage," *Art in America* (July/August 1974): 64–70.

White Marmorean Flock is a term coined by Henry James to describe the "strange sisterhood of American lady sculptors" living in Rome in the nineteenth century. Henry James, *William Wetmore Story and his Friends* (Boston: Houghton, Mifflin & Co, 1903), 257.

1. Jacqueline Fonvielle-Bontemps wrote that Lewis "never sculpted a black figure, though many of the statues dealt with racial or sexual repression as a theme. She glorified abolition as a movement and individual abolitionists, but not black people... Her friends were all white." Fonvielle-Bontemps, *"Forever Free": Art by African American Women, 1862–1980* (Normal, Ill., 1980), 16. Yet another scholar wrote that "where [Lewis's] pieces lose power is in the style she adopted and the material she used: the neo-classical style, with its emphatic focus on Greek idealization, and the pristine whiteness of the marble, which supports the narrowness of the style—so that a black face must appear white and be carved according to the principles of beauty which are white, 'fine' features as perfection." See Michelle Cliff, "Object into Subject: Some Thoughts on the Work of Black Women Artists," in *Visibly Female: Feminism and Art: An Anthology*, ed. Hilary Robinson (London, 1987), 150.

[464] Was the term "stone man" an adaptation of Chippewa or Mohawk language? Richard Rhodes, University of California – Berkeley, Dec. 23, 2010, and Carole Ross, St. Regis Akwesasne Mohawk Tribe, Jan. 11, 2011, say no.

[705] BDET, From Foreign Files, Feb. 3, 1873. For a less influential written insult, see also William Hayes Ackland, unpublished memoirs, Ackland Art Museum, University of North Carolina, Chapel Hill. Ackland, after meeting her at the Centennial, drubbed her as looking like a "southern cook" in a handwritten journal. He later downgraded "cook" to "house maid."

22. Indeed, the only documented plans by Lewis for an Indian sculptural subject that was not drawn from *The Song of Hiawatha* further illustrate her understanding of the potency of these mythic stereotypes. In 1868, Lewis expressed a wish to do a statue of Pocahontas (see L.M. Child to H. Sewall, July 10, 1969 [note 14]), although no evidence exists that it was ever completed.